Colloquial
Korean

The Colloquial Series

Series adviser: Gary King

The following languages are available in the Colloquial series:

Albanian	Korean
Amharic	Latvian
Arabic (Levantine)	Lithuanian
Arabic of Egypt	Malay
Arabic of the Gulf	Mongolian
and Saudi Arabia	Norwegian
Basque	Panjabi
Bulgarian	Persian
* Cambodian	Polish
* Cantonese	Portuguese
* Chinese	Portuguese of Brazil
Croatian and Serbian	Romanian
Czech	* Russian
Danish	Slovak
Dutch	Slovene
Estonian	Somali
Finnish	* Spanish
French	Spanish of Latin America
German	Swedish
Greek	* Thai
Gujarati	Turkish
Hindi	Ukrainian
Hungarian	Urdu
Indonesian	* Vietnamese
Italian	* Welsh
Japanese	

Accompanying cassette(s) (* and CDs) are available for all the above titles. They can be ordered through your bookseller, or send payment with order to Routledge Ltd, ITPS, Cheriton House, North Way, Andover, Hants SP10 5BE, or to Routledge Inc, 29 West 35th Street, New York, NY 10001, USA.

COLLOQUIAL CD-ROMs
Multimedia Language Courses
Available in: Chinese, French, Portuguese and Spanish

Colloquial
Korean

A Complete Language Course

In-Seok Kim

London and New York

First published 1996
by Routledge
11 New Fetter Lane, London EC4P 4EE

Simultaneously published in the USA and Canada
by Routledge
29 West 35th Street, New York, NY 10001

Reprinted in 1997, 2000

Routledge is an imprint of the Taylor & Francis Group

© 1996 In-Seok Kim

Illustrations by Rebecca Moy

Typeset in Times by Graphicraft Typesetters Ltd, Hong Kong

Printed and bound in Great Britain by Clays Ltd, St Ives plc

British Library Cataloguing in Publication Data
A catalogue record for this book is available from the British Library

Library of Congress Cataloguing in Publication Data
A catalogue record for this book is available

ISBN 0-415-10804-7 (book)
ISBN 0-415-10805-5 (cassettes)
ISBN 0-415-10806-3 (book and cassettes course)

Contents

Preface

By the 1980s foreign language education in the United States and Europe had shifted its focus to *doing something* with language rather than *knowing* about it. Many foreign language teachers now hold the view that speaking should be stressed over grammar, even from the very beginning of a language course. In foreign language classes, learners are consistently encouraged to speak in the target language as much as they can, without paying too much attention to the errors they may make. In order to revitalize foreign language instruction and to facilitate this process, instructors have made special efforts to dramatize their classes with a variety of authentic supplementary materials, ranging from newspaper scripts, timetables, and menus, to audio- and videotapes of talkshows by native speakers.

At the heart of this new approach is the concept of "proficiency," which is defined as the student's ability to do something with the language rather than to know about it. This concept is fast becoming the guiding principle around which foreign language curricula and teaching are designed. *Colloquial Korean*, which tries to implement this concept, joins a new breed of functionally based language textbooks.

This self-instructional volume is designed as an elementary language textbook suitable for complete beginners who visit Korea on business, as tourists or who are taking evening classes. However, it can also be used as an excellent supplementary text for Korean language courses offered at university level. The volume provides a broad range of practical situations that enable students to express basic ideas useful in day-to-day living in Korea. It supplies elementary vocabulary and lays the foundation for comprehension of the fundamental principles of Korean grammar. I have endeavored to present material simply and clearly. Different types of oral practice are implemented in a practical context. Vocabulary and grammar

———————————————————————————————

are presented, in a controlled and cumulative manner, throughout the lessons. The pace in presenting the materials is specifically set for those studying on their own. The recordings which come with this book are designed to stimulate enthusiasm, by presenting the authentic sounds of Korean as spoken by native speakers. A complete Answer key, Korean–English/English–Korean glossary, and Grammar index will facilitate the process of learning Korean.

The primary purpose of this volume is to help learners to speak and understand Korean. The approach always emphasizes the ability of learners of Korean to use what they have studied in each lesson, and all materials and activities in the volume are designed to achieve this goal.

Colloquial Korean consists of a tutorial section on Korean sounds and scripts, and twenty lessons. This tutorial is intended to help learners of Korean develop the auditory capability to hear and to discriminate Korean sounds as a learnable system, and to recognize the characters of the Korean alphabet.

Each lesson presents selected dialogues. However, a sentence-by-sentence translation is provided only in the first seven lessons. The eighth lesson serves as a point of departure, after which the learner should feel comfortable with the direct use of the materials without having to rely on English translations. Each lesson has a two-part dialogue, and each part is divided into the following six sections:

Chapter summary This box lays out the major objectives each lesson intends to achieve in terms of topics and grammar points.

Dialogue The Dialogue introduces ten to twelve lines of Korean sentences on a chosen topic. The aim of presenting dramatized dialogues is to familiarize the reader with language materials that are used to express basic ideas in daily conversational forms.

Vocabulary This section lists the key vocabulary items essential to deciphering Korean sentences presented in the dialogues. Some words listed in the Vocabulary or Exercise sections of the previous lessons are re-listed, because they are deemed to be key words or essential to understanding the dialogue or passage concerned.

Grammar points These are devoted to explaining the grammatical patterns in basic terms as well as listing some idiomatic expressions. Both categories are incorporated into the dialogue. Each grammar point is accompanied by several further examples.

Exercises These offer practical material in the patterns of Korean. In working through the exercises, the learner is advised to look up in the Korean–English glossary words not previously introduced or words whose meanings are unfamiliar. However, before you do resort to the glossary, try to deduce the meaning of an unfamiliar word from the context.

Culture point The Culture point section describes some aspect of Korean culture relevant to the theme of the lesson.

Korean letters may look strange, but you'll find after a little practice that you can recognize and reproduce them effortlessly. We will start by looking at the system of Korean sounds and Hangul. Good luck!

Acknowledgments

Colloquial Korean is a self-instructional volume which attempts to integrate my experience of teaching Korean and my research in Korean linguistics with teaching. The volume grew out of its predecessor, *Modern Korean* (first- and second-year course), published in 1990 and 1992, respectively, under grants from the Daewoo Foundation in Seoul, Korea. In publishing *Colloquial Korean*, I am deeply grateful to my former students at Brown University for their input during the experimental phase. I am also grateful to numerous colleagues who have adopted the *Modern Korean* volumes in their Korean language programs, such as the one at Princeton University. Their support and constructive criticism have been greatly appreciated. Without their support this volume, in its present form, could not be published. I am also much indebted to my colleague and long-time friend, Professor Warren Herendeen, in the Department of Language and Communication at Mercy College in Dobbs Ferry, New York, for his warm encouragement and sustained support in many ways. Last, but not least, much credit is due to Simon Bell, Editor in the Language Section at Routledge, who provided me with valuable advice and pedagogical suggestions. I am particularly thankful for the sustained patience and perseverance he has shown to me during the entire course of writing this volume.

Providence, Rhode Island
In-Seok Kim

Introduction: Korean sounds and Hangul

Modern Korean is spoken today throughout the Korean peninsula, the peninsula's total population being over 60 million. Although Korean's linguistic affiliation is debatable, it is commonly believed that it is similar to the Japanese language in terms of pronunciation, structure, and words. Before King Sejong invented the Korean phonetic script Hangul, in 1443, the Korean people had to use as many as 50,000 Chinese characters to make communication possible. At that time Chinese characters were only used by the elite; the majority of the population were excluded from using the Chinese characters, which were extremely difficult to learn and use. In order to revamp the system, King Sejong commissioned his scholars to invent a phonetic script of twenty-eight letters. Since then, Korean people have been using Hangul together with some 12,000 Chinese characters in reading and writing, but they have been pronouncing them in the Korean way, which is quite different from the Chinese pronunciation of corresponding characters. In 1945 the North Korean government abandoned the use of Chinese characters entirely, and the South Korean government made some efforts to phase it out gradually, but failed. In recent years, however, there have been signs that the use of Chinese characters is being encouraged in every walk of Korean society, including elementary, middle, and high schools.

This chapter consists of six Units. It provides a step-by-step presentation of Hangul as a phonetic system and prepares you for learning the material in the lessons that follow. Throughout this section, try to listen to the recording of each Unit over and over again, so that you can develop confidence not only in recognizing Korean sounds but also in pronouncing them in as near-native a way as possible. This confidence will lay the foundation for getting to grips with the dialogues in the lessons. If you don't have the recordings, practice reading the sounds as presented throughout the units.

Unit 1: Vowels 🔲

There are eight simple vowels whose qualities are very different from those of English. These are 아, 어, 오, 우 으, 어, 에, 애.

English approximations

아 is pronounced like "Ah" in "Ah-ha"
어 like "ur" in "fur"
오 like "o" in "tow"
우 like "oo" in "too"
으 like "oo" in "book"
이 like "ee" in "see"
에 like "e" in "pet"
애 like "a" in "pat"

Exercise 1 Circle the vowel you hear:

1 어 어 우 애 에 이
2 으 어 아 오 에 이
3 애 이 에 오 우 으
4 이 아 으 에 오 애
5 어 에 오 이 우 으

Exercise 2 Circle the last vowel you hear:

1 아 우 이 어 애 에
2 우 에 이 오 우 애
3 에 아 이 어 우 애
4 이 오 우 애 에 아
5 애 아 이 어 우 오

Arranging vowels

All Hangul symbols are arranged from top to bottom, as in 오, 우, 으, and from left to right as in 아, 어, 이, 에, 애. Note that when the symbol for a vowel is written, the empty (or zero) consonant "ㅇ" must be added. Each of the eight vowels above is a combination of the zero consonant "ㅇ" and a vowel. Look at the following:

Top   ㅇ   ㅇ   ㅇ
 ↓   ·························
Bottom   ㅗ   ㅜ   ㅡ

Left → Right

ㅇ	ㅏ
ㅇ	ㅓ
ㅇ	ㅣ
ㅇ	ㅔ
ㅇ	ㅐ

Exercise 3 Follow the order of strokes as indicated and write each of the five vowels three times:

LEFT → RIGHT	STROKE NUMBER 1	2	3	4
아	오	이	아	
어	오	오	어	
이	오	이		
에	오	오	어	에
애	오	이	아	애

Exercise 4 Follow the order of strokes as indicated and write each of the three vowels three times:

TOP ↓ BOTTOM	STROKE NUMBER 1	2	3
오	오	오	오
우	오	오	우
으	오	으	

Unit 2: Nine consonants □□

There are nine consonants: ㄱ, ㄴ, ㄷ, ㄹ, ㅁ, ㅂ, ㅅ, ㅇ, ㅈ. Consonant symbols are placed at the beginning of the syllables where the symbol "ㅇ" is found in the vowels (see Unit 1).

1 The first consonant is ㄱ. It is read as "gi-yuk." When we combine this with the vowels, we have:

가 as in "gar" in "gargle"
거 like "gir" in "girl"
고 like "go" in "gore"
구 like "goo" in "goose"
그 like "goo" in "good"
기 like "gi" in "give"
게 like "ge" in "get"
개 like "ga" in "gag"

You write it like this:

So, writing it involves one stroke, moving from left to right and then down.

2 The second consonant is ㄴ. It is read as "ni-un." When we combine this with the vowels, we have:

나 like "nar" in "narcotic"
너 like "ner" in "nerve"
노 like "no" in "nor"
누 like "noo" in "noose"
느 like "noo" in "nook"
니 like "knee"
네 like "ne" in "negative"
내 like "na" in "natty"

You write it like this:

So, writing this consonant involves one stroke, moving from top to bottom and then to the right. The pronunciation of the second consonant should not pose any difficulties for English speakers, since it has the same pronunciation as "n."

3 The third consonant is ㄷ. It is read as "di-gut." When we combine this with the vowels, we get:

다 like "dar" in "darn"
더 like "dir" in "dirt"
도 like "do" in "dog"
두 like "do"
드 like "doo" in "*dook"
디 like "di" in "disk"
데 like "de" in "dedicate"
대 like "da" in "daddy"

   In pronouncing this consonant, the tip of the tongue touches the back of the upper teeth.
   You write it like this:

So, writing this consonant involves two strokes.

4 The fourth consonant is ㄹ. It is read as "ri-ul." When we combine this with the vowels, we have:

라 like "ra" in "rather"
러 like "ru" in "Russia"
로 like "ro" in "robe"
루 like "roo" in "rooster"
르 like "roo" in "rook"
리 like "ri" in "ring"
레 like "re" in "revel"
래 like "ra" in "rat"

Note: An asterisk mark (*) indicates that the word given, aiming to show a sound's Korean pronunciation, cannot be found in English.

In pronouncing this consonant, the tip of the tongue taps lightly against the gum ridge, as it does when you pronounce the word "letter".

You write it like this:

So, writing this consonant involves three strokes.

5 The fifth consonant is ㅁ. It is read as "mi-um." When we combine this with the vowels, we have:

마 like "mar" in "market"
머 like "mer" in "merchant"
모 like "mo" in "mall"
무 like "moo" in "mood"
므 like "moo" in "*mook"
미 like "me"
메 like "me" in "met"
매 like "ma" in "man"

You write it like this:

This symbol is written with three strokes, as shown.

6 The sixth consonant is ㅂ. It is read as "bi-up." When we combine this with the vowels, we have:

바 like "bar"
버 like "bir" in "birth"
보 like "bo" in "bore"
부 like "boo"
브 like "boo" in "book"
비 like "be"
베 like "be" in "best"
배 like "ba" in "bat"

You write this consonant like this:

Four strokes are needed to complete the consonant.

7 The seventh consonant is ㅅ. It is read as "si-os." When we combine this with the vowels, we have:

사 like "sar" in "sardine"
서 like "sur" in "surf"
소 like "sa" in "saw"
수 like "soo" in "soothe"
스 like "soo" in "soot"
시 like "ci" in "city"
세 like "se" in "send"
새 like "sa" in "sand"

You write it like this:

This symbol is written with two strokes.

8 The eighth consonant is ㅇ. It is read as "i-ung" and is an empty consonant, which is placed before any vowel. When the symbol ㅇ is placed at the end of a syllable, its pronunciation is converted to "ng" as in the English word "ink."

You write it like this:

So, writing this consonant involves a single stroke.

9 The final consonant is ㅈ, which is read as "ji-us." When it is combined with the vowels, we get:

자 like "jar"
저 like "jer" in "jerk"
조 like "Joe"
주 like "jui" in "juice"
즈 like "joo" in "*jook"
지 like "ji" in "jig"
제 like "je" in "jelly"
재 like "ja" in "jam"

You can write it in two ways:

 or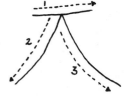

So, writing this symbol involves either two or three strokes.

Exercise 5 🔲 Practice pronouncing the following syllables and compare them with the model pronunciations on the recording:

1 가
2 나
3 주
4 라
5 마
6 사
7 아
8 자
9 제
10 보

Exercise 6 Practice writing out the following combinations in the columns given. As you are writing, try to pronounce each combination clearly and loudly.

1 저									
2 너									
3 노									
4 도									
5 대									
6 르									
7 레									
8 러									
9 모									
10 므									
11 바									
12 브									
13 사									
14 서									
15 공									
16 자									
17 제									
18 지									
19 저									
20 즈									

Exercise 7 🔲 Circle the written syllable or word that you hear on the recording:

1 가 너
2 버 베
3 다 러
4 저 소
5 재주 제주

Exercise 8 🔲 Circle the pair of syllables you hear consecutively:

1 새 가 모 조 바
2 공 강 동 장 송
3 니 베 드 소 머
4 바 다 저 리 조 미
5 에 다 드 누 저 자

Exercise 9 🔲 Write or complete the written syllable that you hear:

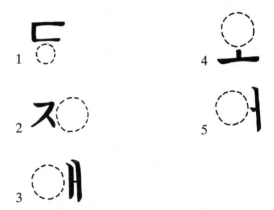

Unit 3: Diphthongs 🔲

A diphthong is a combination of semi-vowels (like Y and W vowels) and a vowel. There are thirteen diphthongs. They are composed of six Y vowels and seven W vowels. You can pronounce these sounds by blowing air out of the lung more tensely than you do when pronouncing the simple vowels. Their pronunciation is completed somewhat quickly, while the tongue moves in the direction of the Y or W vowels. But note that the tongue does not go all the way up to the part of the mouth where these two vowels are produced.

1 The six Y vowels are 야 (아), 애 (애), 여 (어), 예 (에), 요 (오), 유 (우). They are derived from six of the eight simple vowels, as shown in parentheses. These are pronounced close to the English pronunciations:

"ya" in "yard" (야)
"ya" in "yank" (애)
"yu" in "yummy" (여)
"ye" in "yes" (예)
"yo" in "yodel" (요)
"you" (유)

(The simple vowels 으 and 이 are not combined to produce the Y vowel.) An additional stroke on each diphthong signals the Y vowel quality of the sound. This is shown in the following:

$$ 아 + ^- \rightarrow 야 + | \rightarrow 애 $$

$$ 어 + ^- \rightarrow 여 + | \rightarrow 예 $$

$$ 오 + | \rightarrow 요 $$

$$ 우 + | \rightarrow 유 $$

All of these Y vowels, except ㅑ, can be combined with some of the nine consonants (see Unit 2), e.g., 계, 교, 뇨, 려, 묘, 벼, 셔.

Exercise 10 Circle the syllables you hear:

1 가-갸
2 겨-구
3 며-져
4 배-베
5 려-러
6 먀-마
7 가-교
8 조-재
9 라-료
10 고-겨

Exercise 11 🔲 Circle the words you hear:

1 야구-아구
2 교사-고사
3 어유-여유
4 어자-여자
5 여우-어우
6 오리-요리
7 여사-예사
8 조서-주셔
9 자유-자우
10 애기-야기

2 The seven W vowels are 와 (오 + 아), 워 (우 + 어), 외 (오 + 이), 위 (우 + 이), 왜 (오 + 애), 웨 (우 + 에), 의 (으 + 이). These vowels are formed by combining two simple vowels, as shown in parentheses. These are pronounced close to the English pronunciations:

"wa" in "want" (와)
"were" (워)
"way" (외)
"wi" in "wing" (위)
"wa" in "wag" (왜, 웨)
"uy" (의) (closest approximation as in "prune")

All W vowels except ㅒ can be combined with some of the nine consonants (see Unit 2). Some examples are 뭐, 줘, 봐, 솨, 쇄.

3 So far, we have dealt with only the syllables that begin with a consonant. However, the consonants can also occur at the end of a syllable, as schematized in the following two combinations (where C = consonant and V = vowel):

범 $\left(\begin{smallmatrix} CV \\ C \end{smallmatrix}\right)$ 붕 $\left(\begin{smallmatrix} C \\ V \\ C \end{smallmatrix}\right)$

Other common words are 번-분, 건-곤, 잔-존, 천-춘.

Placing a consonant at the end of a syllable may be accompanied by some necessary phonetic change. It is not observable when it comes at the beginning. The following words show types of such phonetic change.

(1) 달, 불, 골   The consonant ㄹ in each syllable is pronounced like "l" as in the English word "hill."

(2) 벽, 적, 목   The consonants ㄱ, ㄷ, ㅂ in these nine syllables

    벋, 맏, 곧   are not released as they are in English words such as "took,"

    법, 접, 몹   "pop," "boot," etc.

(3) 벋, 맏, 곧   The consonants ㅅ, ㅈ in these nine syllables are

    벗, 맛, 곳   pronounced as ㄷ at the end of the word.

    빛, 낮, 젖

(4) 벙, 멍, 정   The consonant ㅇ is pronounced "ng" as in the English word "ink."

Exercise 12   ◖◗   Practice pronouncing the following and compare them with the model pronunciations on the recording:

1 봐   2 죤   3 본   4 꽈   5 뷔
6 쟌   7 꾜   8 뒤   9 뢰   10 솨

Exercise 13 Practice writing the following ten times:

1 냐									
2 려									
3 꽈									
4 솨									
5 눠									
6 뻬									
7 뇌									
8 좌									
9 뉘									
10 놔									

Exercise 14 🔲 Circle the syllable you hear:

1 뒈-꿰
2 쇠-쉬
3 과-귀
4 뵈-뷔
5 봐-쉐
6 뇌-뉘
7 봐-쉬
8 죄-쥐
9 뤼-뢰
10 의-웨

Exercise 15 🔲 Circle the word you hear:

1 감자-겨자
2 종이-문이
3 선박-전갈
4 실력-양력
5 벽지-병지
6 술병-나물
7 지갑-객석
8 야망-달력
9 고개-날개
10 육지-양복

Exercise 16 🔲 Complete the unfinished syllables or words you hear:

1 도
2 ㅎ
3 조

4 역
5 장 ㅁ

Unit 4: Aspirated consonants

The second group of consonants is composed of aspirated consonants ㅊ, ㅋ, ㅌ, ㅍ. Aspirated sounds are the ones produced when
you puff out the air out of your mouth heavily. An initial consonant in each word should be emphasized, as in "car," "take," "paid,"
"church." Note that corresponding words "*gar," "date," "bade,"
"judge" are not aspirated, because a heavy puff of air does not
accompany their pronunciation. These aspirated consonants are
formed by modifying the symbols for the plain consonants "ㅈ, ㄱ,
ㄷ, ㅂ" in the corresponding order, as shown below.

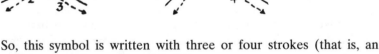

1 The first aspirated consonant is ㅊ. It is read as "chi-us" and is
pronounced as "ch" in "church," e.g., 촌, 천, 쵸, 추, 체.
You write it like this:

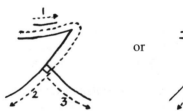

or

So, this symbol is written with three or four strokes (that is, an
additional stroke on the plain ㅈ).

2 The second aspirated consonant is ㅋ. It is read as "ki-uk" and
is pronounced as "k" in "car," e.g., 커, 큰, 켜, 카.
You write it like this:

So, writing the symbol requires two strokes to be completed (that
is, an additional stroke on ㄱ).

3 The third aspirated consonant is ㅌ. It is read as "ti-ut" and is pronounced as "t" in "toy," e.g., 토, 터, 테, 투.
   You write it like this:

So, it requires three strokes to complete (one additional stroke on ㄷ).

4 The fourth aspirated consonant is ㅍ. It is read as "pi-up" and is pronounced as "p" in "pay," as in 포, 폐, 파, 표.
   You write it like this:

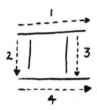

So, this symbol requires four strokes. It can be combined with not only some simple vowels (see Unit 1), but also some diphthongs (see Unit 3).

5 The consonant symbol ㅎ is pronounced "h" as in the English word "hike," which is produced by narrowing the distance between the vocal cords. This symbol requires three strokes to write and causes ㄱ, ㄷ, ㅂ, ㅈ to become aspirated.
   You write it like this:

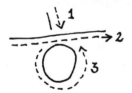

Exercise 17 🔲 Practice pronouncing the following and compare them with the model pronunciations on the recordings:

1 처
2 책

3 컴
4 콩
5 칼
6 탈
7 털
8 풍
9 팻
10 형

Exercise 18 Practice writing the following ten times:

1 처										
2 총										
3 커										
4 캄										
5 텅										
6 튀										
7 테										
8 퍄										
9 평										
10 힝										

Exercise 19 　　 Circle the syllable or word you hear:

1 종-총
2 벙-펑
3 칙-직
4 자리-차리
5 다방-타방
6 바리-파리
7 자리-차리
8 벌덕-팔덕
9 현대-헌대
10 후기-추기

Exercise 20 🔲 Circle two syllables you hear consecutively:

1 란 냇 람 몇 개
2 집 침 잿 개 덴
3 회 의 장 명 팁
4 몽 냇 빛 맷 말
5 캥 거 루 담 택

Exercise 21 🔲 Complete the unfinished syllables as you listen to them:

1 엇

2 요

3 오

4 벼

5 척

Exercise 22 🔲 Write down the syllables or words as you listen to them:

1
2
3

Unit 5: Double consonants 🔲

Certain plain consonants can be doubled (repeated) to produce double consonants. These are ㄲ, ㄸ, ㅃ, ㅆ, ㅉ, and are derived from the plain consonants ㄱ, ㄷ, ㅂ, ㅅ, ㅈ, respectively. The doubling process is shown in the following:

ㄱ	+	ㄱ	→	ㄲ
ㄷ	+	ㄷ	→	ㄸ
ㅂ	+	ㅂ	→	ㅃ
ㅅ	+	ㅅ	→	ㅆ
ㅈ	+	ㅈ	→	ㅉ

The double consonants are pronounced by holding one's mouth tense and then suddenly releasing the sound without aspiration. The pronounciation of each double consonant is closest to "k" in "sky" (ㄲ), "t" in "stick" (ㄸ), "p" in "spy" (ㅃ), "s" in "sink" (ㅆ), and "t" in "cuts" (ㅉ). Another group of double consonants may come at the end of a syllable. These consonants are

ㅄ, ㄿ, ㄽ, ㄳ, ㄶ, ㄺ, ㄻ, ㄼ, ㄾ, ㅀ

all of which combine two different consonants. However, only one of these two consonants is pronounced, the knowledge of which one can come to grips with in the course of learning Korean. The double consonants ㄲ and ㅆ can also come finally, and they are pronounced like their corresponding plain consonants ㄱ, ㅅ. The following examples show which consonant is pronounced and which is not:

밖 (박)	핥 (할)	밝 (박)
싫 (실)	넋 (넉)	값 (갑)
앉 (안)	읊 (읖)	많 (만)
돐 (돌)	굶 (굼)	었 (엇)
짧 (짭)		

Exercise 23 Practice pronouncing the following:

1 깔	6 때	11 짜
2 꼴	7 빨	12 쯔
3 꿍	8 뿌	13 짝
4 뚱	9 썰	14 쪽
5 뜻	10 씀	15 쯤

Exercise 24 Practice writing the following ten times:

1 꾸										
2 꿍										
3 떵										
4 또										
5 뻘										
6 빰										
7 뿌										
8 썰										
9 쩔										
10 짝										
11 낄										
12 쏘										
13 끌										
14 쫑										
15 똑										

Exercise 25 🔊 Circle the syllable you hear:

1 거-꺼
2 구-꾸
3 또-도
4 돌-똘
5 봉-뽕
6 더-떠
7 돌-딸

8 검-껌
9 갈-깔
10 달-딸

Exercise 26 🔘🔘 Circle the word you hear:

1 가다-까다
2 끄다-그다
3 꼬다-고다
4 달랑-딸랑
5 긍긍-끙끙
6 조석-쪼석
7 잘다-짤다
8 적적-쩍쩍
9 부다-푸다
10 서다-쓰다

Exercise 27 🔘🔘 Circle the word you hear:

1 가다-카다-까다
2 그다-크다-끄다
3 고다-코다-꼬다
4 달랑-탈랑-딸랑
5 긍긍-킁킁-끙끙
6 종-총-쫑
7 잘다-찰다-짤다
8 자다-차다-짜다
9 굴-쿨-꿀
10 부다-푸다-뿌다

Exercise 28 🔘🔘 Complete the unfinished syllable that corresponds to each one you hear:

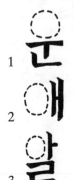

1 운
2 애
3 알

4

5

Unit 6: Summary, word structure, and other aspects of Korean

1 Modern Korean uses 40 sounds, consisting of 8 simple vowels, 13 diphthongs, and 19 consonants, as shown in the following summary chart:

Simple vowels		아	어	오	우	으	이	에	애
Diphthongs	Y vowels	야	여	요	유	애	예		
	W vowels	와	워	외	위	왜	웨	의	
Consonants	plain	ㄱ	ㄴ	ㄷ	ㄹ	ㅁ	ㅂ	ㅅ	ㅇ ㅈ
	aspirated	ㅊ	ㅋ	ㅌ	ㅍ	ㅎ			
	double	ㄲ	ㄸ	ㅃ	ㅆ	ㅉ			

2 The following Korean alphabet chart shows all the possible combinations between 10 major vowels and diphthongs selected and 14 consonants (except double consonants). This means that all of these are allowable combinations, but the ones that are marked * are not used. Since it is not always easy for even a native speaker of Korean to distinguish between possible combinations and impossible ones, learners are advised to study the possible combinations of these as they come across them in the sentences presented in this book.

Korean alphabet chart

	Vowel/diphthong									
	아	야	어	여	오	요	우	유	으	이
Consonant										
ㄱ	가	*갸	거	겨	고	교	구	규	그	기
ㄴ	나	*냐	너	녀	노	뇨	누	뉴	느	니
ㄷ	다	*댜	더	*뎌	도	*됴	두	*듀	드	디
ㄹ	라	*랴	러	려	로	료	루	류	르	리
ㅁ	마	*먀	머	며	모	묘	무	*뮤	므	미
ㅂ	바	*뱌	버	벼	보	*뵤	부	*뷰	브	비
ㅅ	사	*샤	서	셔	소	*쇼	수	*슈	스	시
ㅇ	아	*야	어	여	오	요	우	유	으	이
ㅈ	자	*쟈	저	져	조	죠	주	*쥬	즈	지
ㅊ	차	*챠	처	쳐	초	*쵸	추	*츄	츠	치
ㅋ	카	*캬	커	켜	코	*쿄	쿠	*큐	크	키
ㅌ	타	*탸	터	*텨	토	*툐	투	*튜	트	티
ㅍ	파	*퍄	퍼	펴	포	표	푸	*퓨	프	피
ㅎ	하	*햐	허	혀	호	효	후	휴	흐	히

Note: An asterisk (*) indicates impossible combinations (and therefore not used in Modern Korean), but some of these can be used for words borrowed from many foreign languages including English.

Only some of other remaining vowels and diphthongs can be combined with the consonants, including double consonants, as in: 좌, 봐, 뷔, 워, 좌, 꿔, 꽈, 꼬, 깨.

3 A Korean letter is made up of three parts: initial, medial, and final. The first two parts are composed of either a vowel or diphthong sound, while the last only consists of the consonant (including the zero consonant ㅇ). There are three types of combinations that can occur.

3.1 All letters in the above chart show a series of two-part letters. When we place the consonant (let's say ㄱ) of the three-part letters underneath the letters of the first line in the column (which is already the combination of a consonant ㄱ and a vowel ㅏ), we get the ten full letters 각, *갹, 걱, 격, 곡, *굑 , 국, *귝, 극, 긱. However, letters that are marked * among these are not possible letters, the knowledge of which again belongs to the area of the native speaker's intuition. We can do the same combination again with a series of letters on the first line in the column. By placing the arbitrary consonant ㄷ vertically underneath them, we get another ten full letters on the first line of the column, only three of which are used in Modern Korean: 건, 곤, 군. By placing other consonants and even aspirated and double consonants underneath the letters on the chart, we can get the other full letters in use. Some of them are: 공, 농, 눌, 강, 랑, 돈, 찾, 엌.

3.2 When we place the third consonant (say ㄱ) underneath the combined letter (e.g., 과) of a consonant (ㄱ) and a diphthong (와), we then get the full letter 곽. Likewise, we can get many other three-part full letters which are: 권, 퀸, 쉰, 쉰, 쾡. Here again, the learner is advised to learn three-part full letters using the diphthongs, as they occur in the sentences in the book.

3.3 Double consonants can also fill the third position, forming a full letter. These letters are: 있, 묶, 샀. And yet two different consonants can fill the third position as in 앉, 돐, 없, 값, etc. As explained in Unit 5, only one representative consonant is actually pronounced. Words of the first group above are pronounced as if they were 잇, 묵, 삿, while words of the second group are pronounced as if they were 안, 돌, 업, 갑.

4 Word structure Korean words are usually built out of combining a number of letters, the process of which we have seen above. For example, the word 가다 has two letters and is used as a verb meaning "go." There are also longer words than this such as 모르다 "do not know," 인사하다 "greet." However, even a limited number of single letters can be used as if they were words: 강 "river," 눈 "eyes," 집 "house," etc.

5 Stress and intonation Unlike English, Korean employs neither a word stress (sometimes called accent) nor a sentence stress. Every English word puts an emphasis on one of its syllables (like on the first syllable in "hístory") whereas every Korean word sounds flat and regular. Furthermore, Korean sentences do not receive any stress, unlike English sentences (e.g., 'The báby is ínterested in pláying with a tóy"). Because of this, to an English-speaking person, the rhythm of Korean sounds very mechanical, where sounds are lined up together with equal force and at regular intervals. However, Korean employs three kinds of intonation at the end of a sentence:

rising, falling, falling and momentary sustenance. The first type is used for statements, whereas the second type is for questions. The last type is used for commands and requests. The difference between them will be explained in detail in Lesson 2.

6 Punctuation The Korean language uses three kinds of punctuation mark at the end of a sentence. These are the period (.), the question mark (?), and the exclamation point (!). The comma (,) and other separators – the colon (:), semicolon (;), and the dash (-) – are also used within a sentence. Quotation marks (" ", ' ') are often used to enclose the exact words of a speaker or writer. The usage of all these punctuation marks is very similar to that of English and other languages.

Korean alphabet bingo game ▢▢

Directions

Write down in the box on p.26 any sixteen of the thirty-five Korean letters given below. While the instructor on the recording calls the letters in random order, cross out the letters you have written when you hear them called. If you cross out four letters in a row – in a vertical, horizontal, or diagonal direction – you can call "bingo." Then, you may stop the recording and check them against the model answer (see Key to exercises in the back of the book).

가	거	뉴	디	유	요	추
처	토	표	푸	휴	히	치
루	로	차	카	파	하	냐
벼	머	커	마	공	쌀	뚱
깔	꺼	삐	빨	찌	짝	쪽

Should it turn out that all four words are lined up in any of the three directions, you are a real bingo winner. Congratulations! You have at last mastered the Korean alphabet system. Now you may proceed to Lesson 1.

1 인사
Greetings

By the end of this lesson you should be able to:
- greet someone properly in Korean
- address Korean adults
- write Korean names
- use the sentence ending -세요
- use the negative marker 안
- use the postposition -에
- use the topic case marker -은/는

Dialogue 1 ◨◧ *Mr. Kim and Miss Lee, colleagues in the office, casually greet each other on the street after not having seen each other for some time. This kind of greeting may occur at any time of day and in any situation. Mr. Kim also asks about one of their other colleagues, Mr. Park*

KIM: 안녕하세요?
LEE: 김선생님 안녕하세요?
KIM: 오래간만입니다.
LEE: 예, 오래간만입니다.
KIM: 요즈음 어떻게 지내세요?
LEE: 잘 지냅니다.
KIM: 박선생님은 어떠세요?
LEE: 박선생님 잘 지내세요.

KIM: *How are you?*
LEE: *How are you, Mr. Kim?*
KIM: *It's been a long time since I saw you.*
LEE: *Yes, it has.*
KIM: *How is everything with you these days?*
LEE: *I'm doing all right.*
KIM: *How about Mr. Park?*
LEE: *He's doing all right.*

Vocabulary

안녕	peace	입니다	is, are
하다	do	어떻게	how
안녕하세요?	How are you?	지내다	get along
미스터	Mr.	잘	well
미스	Ms., Miss	은-는	as for . . .
예	yes	요즈음	these days
오래간만	long time		

Language points

Asking "How are you?"

Most phrases introduced in this dialogue are idiomatic expressions which do not require further analysis. For example, the phrase 안녕하세요? literally means "Are you in peace?" but it is functionally translated into the English expression "How are you?" Thus, these expressions should be learned as set phrases.

Addressing Korean adults

Koreans rarely address anyone by name without using an appropriate title. They use a job-related title alone or with a last name, after which a noun suffix 님 is attached, indicating respect shown to the person. When the person's job-related title is not clear, they commonly use 선생님 ("teacher" plus honorific noun suffix), with his/her last name.

Examples using job-related titles		Examples using last names	
선생님	teacher	김선생님	Mr. Kim
교수님	professor	이선생님	Mr. Lee
의사 선생님	medical doctor	박선생님	Mr. Park
김박사님	Dr. Kim (Ph.D. degree)	최선생님	Mr. Choi
과장님	section chief		
사장님	president		

However, when a senior employee of an organization addresses a relatively new employee (especially a high school or college graduate) whose status (or age) is lower than his, English loan words 미스터 (for a male) and 미스 (for a female) can be used. This way of addressing employees is widely practiced especially in modern firms in Korea.

미스터 김 Mr. Kim
미스터 송 Mr. Song
미스 나 Miss Na
미스 한 Miss Han

Writing Korean names

The full Korean name takes the order of last name first, first name second as in:

김달수 Dal Soo Kim
한근수 Geun Soo Han
조재걸 Jae Gul Jo

Other typical expressions

Other ways of responding to the expression 요즈음 어떻게 지내세요? are as follows:

그저 그래요   So-so
좋아요   Good
잘 지냅니다.   I'm doing all right.
바쁘게 지냅니다.   I am busy.

Polite expression for "How are you?"

When people meet each other for the first time, they tend to use a more polite expression 안녕하십니까? In this case, both parties usually use a title of respect (선생 "teacher" in its literal sense) combined with an honorific marker 님. The junior person may also use this expression to the senior in a greeting to show more respect.

윤선생님, 안녕하십니까? Mr. Yoon, how are you?
김선생님, 안녕하십니까? I'm fine. How about you, Mr. Kim?

Topic case marker - 은/는

When an element of a sentence introduces a new topic in comparison with something talked about in the previous sentence, the
suffix - 은 is attached to the element ending in a consonant, but the
suffix - 는 is added to the element ending in a vowel. This topic
case marker means roughly "As for . . ."

박선생님은 안녕하세요.   Mr. Park is OK.
이선생님은 잘 지내세요.   Mr. Lee is doing well.
미스 리는 잘 지내세요.   Miss Lee is doing well.
미스 최는 잘 지내세요.   Miss Choi is doing well.

Exercises

1 Greet the following colleagues whom you run across on the streets
of Seoul.

a Mr. Kim
b Professor Lee
c Section Chief Park
d Miss Kang

2 Greet the following people you are meeting for the first time.

a Mr. Kim (M.D.)
b President of the company
c Miss Chang (teacher)

3 Someone asks you how everything is with you these days. Respond
to the question with the following:

a I'm doing OK.
b So-so.
c These days, I'm busy.

4 Rearrange the words of the dialogue to make sense.

a 오래, 입니다. 예, 간만
b 리, 미스, 하세요? 안녕
c 지내세요? 요즈음, 어떻게
d 교수님, 하십니까? 안녕, 김

5 Pronounce and write the following names in Korean.

a Ki Soo Kang
b Sang Dal Park
c Keun Young Kim

6 You are the president of a Korean company which has recently hired a number of new staff members. How would you address the following staff when you run across them in the hallway?

a Mr. Kim
b Ms. Han
c Miss Na
d Mr. Shin

7 Ask a colleague how the following are doing at the moment (these days):

a Mr. Jin
b Miss Hwang
c Section Chief Park
d Ms. Lee (your junior)

Culture point
The basic concepts which underlie the deferential system of the Korean language are rooted in Confucian ethics. The tenets of this ancient Chinese philosophy dictate three beliefs: 1, one person may be more powerful than another; 2, one may be older than another; 3, one may be lower in social rank than another. The one who is deemed more powerful, older, and higher in social rank receives corresponding respect through the language used. This is the reason the Korean language is full of honorific vocabulary and expressions, the use of which often baffles the learner. Those learning Korean must understand that Koreans do not usually honor equality in their daily interpersonal relationships. Instead, a sense of inequality permeates the Korean language, and a speaker has to find an appropriate social rank or right age of the other person in order to communicate with him or her in the proper manner. When using 미스터 and 미스, which are English-influenced terms of address, one should address them neither to people with whom one is not very familiar nor to people more powerful and/or older than oneself.

Dialogue 2 📼 *Mr. Kim and Miss Lee exchange the following short greetings when they pass. They may or may not have met once during the day*

KIM: 이선생님, 바쁘세요?
LEE: 예, 좀 바빠요. 김선생님은 어떠세요?
KIM: 저는 별로 안 바빠요.
LEE: 지금 어디 가세요?
KIM: 우체국에 갑니다.
     이선생님은 어디 가세요?
LEE: 저는 식당에 갑니다.
KIM: 그럼, 안녕히 가세요.
LEE: 예, 안녕히 가세요.

KIM: Are you busy, Mr. Lee?
LEE: Yes, I am a little busy. And you?
KIM: I'm not very busy.
LEE: Where are you going now?
KIM: I'm going to the post office.
     Where are you going?
LEE: I'm going to a restaurant.
KIM: Well, goodbye then.
LEE: Bye.

Vocabulary

바쁘세요	busy	식당	restaurant
좀	a little	그럼	well, then
별로	particularly	안녕히	peacefully
안	not	저는	as for me (humble expression)
가세요	go		
갑니다	go	우체국	post office
지금	now		
어디	where		

Language points

Sentence ending -세요

This sentence ending, as attached to the verb stem, is used to express a statement with falling intonation, a question with rising intonation, and a request with momentarily sustained and falling intonation. The honorific marker -세 indicates respect shown to the listener who is older or higher in social status than the speaker.

Verb stem	Sentence ending (honorific)
바쁘다 busy	바쁘세요
가다 go	가세요
어떻다 how	어떠세요
지금 바쁘세요?	Are you busy now?
이선생님 지금 바쁘세요.	Mr. Lee is busy now.

The negative marker -안

This marker negates most Korean verbs except identification verbs (which will be introduced at a later stage) when it is placed before a verb.

박선생님은 바쁘세요.	Mr. Park is busy.
박선생님은 안 바쁘세요.	Mr. Park isn't busy.
이선생님은 교회에 가세요.	Mr. Lee goes to church.
이선생님은 교회에 안 가세요.	Mr. Lee doesn't go to church.

The manner adverb 별로

This can also be used only with the negative marker 안 or other forms of negation (i.e., -지 않다) in the sentence.

지금 별로 안 바빠요.	I am not very busy.
별로 안 좋아요.	I am not very well.

The postposition -에

This postposition is attached directly to a place word and is followed by 가다 "go," or 오다 "come", or their compound verbs. It refers to a specific direction.

교회에 갑니다.	(I) am going to church.
도서관에 갑니다.	(I) am going to the library.
집에 갑니다.	(I) am going home.
오늘 교회에 오세요.	Please come to church today.

Exercises

8 Assume that your father is going to the following places and that someone asks where he is going. Answer the question using -세요?

a church
b library
c restaurant
d post office

9 Someone asks if you are going to the following places. Answer the question in the negative.

a church
b library
c home
d post office

10 You are helping a friend with their Korean grammar. Correct the mistakes in these sentences.

a 강선생님은 안 별로 바쁘세요.
b 미스터 리는 별로 좋으세요.
c 미스 진은 안 교회에 가세요.
d 최교수님은 도서관에 별로 가세요.

2 친구 소개하기
Introducing friends

By the end of this lesson you should be able to:
- introduce your friend(s) to a third party in different settings
- say goodbye to one another
- use three forms of expressions: declarative, interrogative, and request
- use personal pronouns (e.g., 나, 너, 그, etc.)
- use the subject case markers -이/가
- use the future tense -겠

Dialogue 1 🔲 *Mr. Kim introduces one of his friends, Mary Jin, to Mr. Kang at the end-of-the-year party*

KIM: 진 선생님, 안녕하세요?
KANG: 예, 김 선생님, 안녕하세요?
KIM: 요즈음 어떻게 지내세요?
KANG: 덕택에 잘 지냅니다.
KIM: 강 선생님, 제 친구 소개하겠습니다.
　　　이분이 메리 진씨입니다.
JIN: 처음 뵙겠습니다. 저 메리 진입니다.
KANG: 처음 뵙겠습니다. 저 강기수입니다.

KIM: *Miss Jin. How are you?*
KANG: *I'm fine. Mr. Kim. How are you?*
KIM: *How are you getting along these days?*
KANG: *I'm doing fine, thanks to you.*
KIM: *Mr. Kang. Let me introduce my friend to you.*
　　　This is Mary Jin.
JIN: *Nice to meet you. I'm Mary Jin.*
KANG: *Nice to meet you. I'm Ki Soo Kang.*

Vocabulary

덕택에	thanks (to you)	이분	this person
친구	friend	처음	first time
소개하다	introduce	뵙다	see (humble form)
제	my	씨	Mr. or Miss

Language points

Forms of expression

Korean sentences use five forms of expression: 1 declarative, 2 interrogative, 3 request, 4 command, and 5 exclamation. These forms of expression are determined by their verb ending and intonation.
  Here are examples of the first three types:

Declarative

오래간만입니다.	It's been a long time since I last saw you.
처음 뵙겠습니다.	I'm glad to meet you.
이제 가봐야겠습니다.	I must be going now.
안 바빠요.	I'm not busy.

Interrogative

안녕하십니까?	How are you?
메리 스미쓰입니까?	Are you Mary Smith?
이분 아세요?	Do you know this person?
바쁘세요?	Are you busy?

Request

안녕히 가십시오.	Bye-bye (*lit.* please go in peace).
안녕히 계십시오.	Bye-bye (*lit.* please stay in peace).
인사하세요.	Please say hello.

Examples for commands and exclamations will be introduced later.

The verb ending - 입니다, - 습니다 is exclusively used in declarative sentences, but the verb ending - 입니까?, 습니까? is used for interrogative sentences. However, the verb ending - 십시오 is limited to a request. The ending - 요 can be used, with varying intonation, to form more than one kind of expression.

Linking verb -입니다

The linking verb -입니다 is a verb that identifies the predicate of a sentence with the subject, the function of which is to link the subject and predicate.

Subject	Predicate
이분이	강기수씨-입니다.
이분이	강기수씨-입니까?

Note that the English verb "to be" ("am," "are," "is") is incorporated into Korean predicate endings by using -입니다. It must always be attached to the preceding noun.

이분이	한기수씨	입니다.
This person	Ki Soo Han	+ is

Subject case markers -이/가

Korean uses the subject case marker -이 after words ending in a consonant and -가 after those ending in a vowel. The systematic use of case markers in Korean such as these is rather complex, so this topic will be gradually expanded in the forthcoming lessons.

Words ending in a consonant	Words ending in a vowel
이분이	한기수씨가
저사람이	내가
책이	우리가
책상이	친구가

The future tense marker -겠

The future tense marker, inserted between the verb stem and the ending, indicates an action that takes place in the future, or a condition, or quality which will exist at some other time.

홍차 한잔 하겠어요.	I'd like to drink a cup of tea.
공부하겠어요.	I'll study.
지금 가겠어요.	I'll go now.
내일 오겠어요.	I'll come tomorrow.

Exercises

1 You are on the phone and the person at the other end of the line asks who you are. Respond to the question.

2 Using the vocabulary given, answer the question 이분이 누구입니까?

a Mary Jin
b Professor Kim
c Mary Smith

3 Read the following English words and choose an appropriate subject case marker suitable for their Korean equivalents.

a we
b my friend
c desk

4 One of your friends thinks you're going to be busy with several activities over the weekend and asks what you are going to do. Respond to his questions.

a go to church
b study
c go to the library

5 Examine the following sentences and write in "D" for declarative sentences, "I" for interrogative sentences, and "R" for request sentences.

a 이분이 강기수씨입니다.
b 안녕하세요?
c 인사하세요.
d 저분 소개하세요.

Culture point

When a Korean introduces someone to a third party, he usually takes him/her to a person who is older, more powerful, and/or senior. The first questions the senior person will ask of the person being introduced are likely to be of a somewhat personal and private nature and may include questions about the younger or less powerful person's age, occupation, marriage, or the number of children he or she is raising. By gleaning this information from the one introduced, the senior or more powerful person can establish not only interpersonal relationships with him/her, but also the register of the language used in communicating with the person being introduced. This kind of "interpersonal relationship" is often carried to an extreme when Koreans meet foreigners for the first time. That is, they rush to ask similar questions of them, although the questions require personal and private answers. Foreigners need to realize that such questions are not intended to make one feel uncomfortable, but are a socially acceptable conversational form. As a preventive measure, one may draw on some sort of wit or wisdom with which to dodge the questions, without looking too evasive!

Dialogue 2 🔲🔲 *Miss Yoon takes one of her colleagues, John Kim, to a party in her friend's house. His name is Ki Soo Kang. Miss Yoon introduces him to Mr. Kang. After having spent some time at the party, John Kim wants to say goodbye to the host*

YOON: 강기수씨, 이분 아세요?
KANG: 아니요, 모릅니다.
YOON: 인사하세요.
　　　이분이 존 김씨입니다.
KIM: 처음 뵙겠습니다.
KANG: 처음 뵙겠습니다.
　　　(저) 강기수입니다.
　　　　(Later)
KIM: 이제 가 봐야겠습니다.
　　　그럼, 다음에 또 뵙겠습니다.
KANG: 안녕히 가십시오.
KIM: 안녕히 계십시오.

YOON: *Mr. Kang. Do you know this person?*
KANG: *No, I don't know him.*
YOON: *Please greet him.*
　　　This is John Kim.
KIM: *Glad to meet you.*
KANG: *Glad to meet you.*
　　　I'm Ki Soo Kang.
　　　　(Later)
KIM: *I must be going now.*
　　　Well, then, I'll be seeing you again.
KANG: *Bye now.*
KIM: *Bye.*

Vocabulary

알다	know	모르다	do not know
아니요	no	다음에	next time
인사하다	greet	또	again
가 보다	try to go		
계십시오	bye-bye		
	(to the person leaving)		

Language points

Basic Korean sentence structure

Korean sentences basically consist of a subject and a predicate. The subject is the part of the sentence which tells you "who" or "what." The predicate is the part of the sentence which tells what someone or something does (or is).

Subject	Predicate
저	메리 진입니다
저	이분 알아요.

One of the characteristics of Korean is that the verb is always placed at the end of the sentence.

	Verb
이분	아세요?
안녕히	가십시오.
제 친구	소개하겠습니다.
	etc.

Another characteristic of Korean is its tendency to omit the subject of a sentence if this is obvious from the context.

Subject	Predicate	
(저)	메리 진입니다.	I'm Mary Jin.
(저)	이분 알아요.	I know her (this person).
(선생님)	이분 아세요?	Do you know her (this person)?

Personal pronouns

Person	Level	Singular	Plural
first	familiar	나/내 I	우리 we
	humble	저/제	저희
second	familiar	너/네 you	너희 you
third	familiar	그 사람 he/she	그 사람들 they
	honorific	그분	그분들

First and second person singular pronouns require specific particles when they are used as the subject of a sentence. Pronouns such
as 나, 저, 너 always take 는 (thus 나는, 저는, 너는), whereas pronouns such as 내, 제, 네 always take 가 (thus 내가, 제가, 네가).
Note that Korean uses honorifics, where a person of high social
status receives respect in speech. One can also indirectly honor the
other person present or a third party absent from the context
by using either very respectful words for them or words lowering
oneself.

Saying goodbye

Korean has distinctive forms for saying goodbye to a remaining or
departing host or hostess. Regardless of whether one is the person
leaving or staying, English speakers use the expressions, "goodbye," "bye-bye," or "so long." In contrast, Korean speakers use
the expression 안녕히 계세요 (*lit.* "stay in peace") to the remaining host or hostess, and use the somewhat different expression
안녕히 가세요 (*lit.* "go in peace") to the departing guest. When
both parties leave, they of course exchange the same, latter, expression 안녕히 가세요.

Exercises

6 Someone asks you whether you know Mr. Lee, who has recently joined the company, and whom you do not know. How would
you respond to the question?

7 Someone asks you whether you know Miss Kang, who became Prime Minister of Korea. You and Miss Kang attended the same college in the United States. How would you respond?

8 You are about to leave a party which is still in full swing. How would you say goodbye to the remaining guests at the party?

9 You have invited several people in the neighborhood. Having had a good time for a while, they are now leaving. How would you say goodbye to them?

10 There are several people at work whom you have to introduce to your roommate. Introduce the following individuals:

a Mr. Kim
b Section Chief Park
c Miss Hwang

11 Choose one word that does not belong to the given group:

a 나, 저, 우리, 너
b 우리, 저희, 너희, 그 사람
c 나, 너, 그 사람, 저희

12 Translate the following expressions, giving their Korean equivalents:

a I'm glad to meet you.
b Please meet him.
c This is Jenny Lee.
d I must be going.
e I'll be seeing you again.

3 사무실에서
In an office

By the end of this lesson you should be able to:
- visit friends at work
- offer a visitor something to drink
- use the endings for a statement, a question, and a request
- use built-in honorific vocabulary
- use honorific insertions -세/시
- use the informal ending -이에요
- use the causal conjunction -아(어/여)서

Dialogue 1 🔲 *Kyung Hee Park has arrived at the office where Mr. Kim works and asks the secretary if he is in*

PARK: 수고하십니다. 김선생님 계세요?
SECRETARY: 네, 누구세요?
PARK: (저) 박경희입니다.
            김선생님(의) 사업친구입니다.
SECRETARY: 잠깐 기다리세요. 이리 앉으세요.
PARK: 네, 감사합니다.
            (*A moment later*)
SECRETARY: 들어가세요.

PARK: *Hello. Is Mr. Kim in?*
SECRETARY: *Yes. May I take your name?*
PARK: *I'm Kyung Hee Park.*
            (I'm) a business friend.
SECRETARY: *Please wait a moment. Have a seat here.*
PARK: *Thank you.*
            (*A moment later*)
SECRETARY: *Please go in.*

Vocabulary

수고하십니다	Hello	기다리다	wait
누구	·who	이리	this way
사업	business	앉다	sit
잠깐	a moment	감사하다	thank
들어가다	enter		

Language points

Two different forms of honorifics

The Korean language makes use of two different forms of honorifics – short and long – when making a statement, asking a question, and making a request. These forms are almost interchangeable and there is almost no difference in meaning between them. The long form, however, is slightly more formal (thus more polite) than the short form (informal). The latter form tends to be used more commonly by women than by men.

Statement with falling intonation
-세요 (short)   -십니다 (long)
바쁘세요.	바쁘십니다.	(Someone) is busy.
기다리세요.	기다리십니다.	(Someone) is waiting.
계세요.	계십니다.	(Someone) is in.

Question with rising intonation
-세요? (short)   -십니까? (long)
바쁘세요?	바쁘십니까?	Are you busy?
		(*or* Is someone busy?)
기다리세요?	기다리십니까?	Are you waiting?
		(*or* Is someone waiting?)
계세요?	계십니까?	Is someone in?

Request with momentary sustenance and falling intonation
-세요 (short)   -십시오 (long)
인사하세요.	인사하십시오.	Please greet.
안녕히 가세요.	안녕히 가십시오.	Please go in peace (Bye-bye).
기다리세요.	기다리십시오.	Please wait.

Built-in honorific verbs

Korean uses a system of built-in honorific verbs, which are separate from the honorific verbs above. These honorific verbs are derivable by inserting either -세 (short form) or -십시 (long form) into a verb stem.

Verb stem	*Honorific form*	
있다	계시다	to exist, to be
자다	주무시다	to sleep
먹다	잡수시다	to eat
말하다	말씀 드리다	to say, tell, speak
보다	뵙다	to see
주다	드리다	to give
묻다	여쭙다	to ask

Interrupting someone at a job site

The expression 수고하십니다 literally means that you are engaged in doing hard work. In lieu of a greeting, you may use this expression when you try to interrupt those engaged in work. However, you cannot use it to a third party absent from the scene.

수고하십니다.	May I interrupt you?
홍선생님 계세요?	Is Mr. Hong in?
아니오, 지금 안 계십니다.	No, he isn't now.

Exercises

1 Write down the following three things you think your father will do today, using the short form ending -세요:

a stay at home
b drink a cup of coffee
c be busy

2 Do the same as in 1, this time using the long form ending -십니다.

3 You have thrown a party for your friends at work and you are offering them a cup of something to drink.

a milk
b beer

c ginseng tea
d soda

4 One of your friends has visited you in the office and your secretary asks him to do the following, while she makes sure you are free to see him:

a have a seat here
b come this way
c go in

5 Translate the following sentences into Korean, using the honorific verb ending -세요:

a Mr. Kim sits over here.
b Miss Lee is sleeping.
c Dr. Chang is going home now.

6 Do the same as in 5, using the honorific verb ending -십니다.

7 Translate the following dialogue:

A: Hello. Is Miss Chang in?
B: Yes, she is in. May I take your name?
A: I am a business friend.
B: Please wait a moment.
A: Thank you.

Culture point
Koreans, as a rule, place great value on their feelings of self-esteem. This feeling is known as "kibun" in Korean, which is not easy to translate into English, although it might be loosely translated as "karma." Koreans feel jubilant when their "kibun" is good. However, they feel gloomy when it is bad. For this reason, a foreigner should be careful not to push Koreans off the edge – not to turn their "kibun" bad – in verbal communication with them. Once their "kibun" feels bad, reaching any agreement with Koreans is very difficult. Of course, this is not to say that a foreigner ought to flatter Koreans in order to maintain successful communications with them, but sometimes a little carelessness on the part of the foreigner may lead to a disastrous situation where the relationship is irrevocably damaged.

Dialogue 2 ▢▢ *Kyung Hee Park and her former business partner, Mr. Kim, exchange greetings and carry on a brief conversation. Mr. Kim offers her a cup of coffee*

PARK: 김선생님, 안녕하세요? 오래간만이에요.
KIM: 네, 오래간만입니다. 여기 앉으세요.
      커피 한 잔 하시겠어요?
PARK: 네, 감사합니다. 김선생님, 요즘 어떻게 지내세요?
KIM: 저는 괜찮습니다. 박선생님은 어떠세요?
PARK: 바쁘게 지냅니다. 요즘 장사가 잘 돼서 기분이 좋아요.
KIM: 참, 좋으시겠어요.

PARK: *Mr. Kim, how are you? It's been a long time since I saw you.*
KIM: *Yes, it's been a long time. Have a seat here.*
      Would you like a cup of coffee?
PARK: *Yes, thank you. Mr. Kim, how's everything with you these days?*
KIM: *I'm okay. How about you, Mr. Park?*
PARK: *I'm really busy. And my business is doing well, so I'm in a good mood.*
KIM: *You must be really happy.*

Vocabulary

바쁘게	busily	- 이에요, 입니다	is, are
장사	business	예, 네	yes
기분	mood, spirits	여기	here
좋다	good	커피	coffee
잘 되다	doing well	한 잔	one cup
오래간만	long time	괜찮다	OK
요즘	lately	참, 정말로	really

Language points

The informal ending - 이에요

A non-honorific long ending - 입니다 is often pronounced as - 이에요 and spelled in this way. Female speakers and school-children tend to adopt this pronunciation, but male speakers prefer to use its original form. When the sentence ending - 이에요 comes after a noun ending in a vowel, the vowel 이 is usually contracted to the following vowel 에, resulting in a single syllable 에.

저 사람은 학생이에요.   The person is a student.
그분은 강철민씨예요.   He's Chul Min Kang.

The adverbial ending -게

Attached to certain adjectives, this ending makes the adjective into
an adverb.

빠르다	빠르게	quickly
느리다	느리게	slowly
바쁘다	바쁘게	busily

The conjunction -아(어/여)서

This conjunction is used to indicate a causal relationship between
two combined sentences. It is directly attached to the stem of the
fist action verb and is followed by the second verb.

오늘은 바빠서, 도서관에 안   Since I'm busy today, I am
  가요.   not going to the library.
눈이 많이 와서, 교회에 안   Since it has snowed a lot, I
  가요.   am not going to church.
피곤해서, 자겠어요.   Since I'm tired, I am going
                                  to sleep.

The possessive marker -의

This particle indicates possession: it is equivalent to the English
"'s" and "of." The first noun with the particle modifies the second
noun. In casual conversations, the possessive marker -의 is usually deleted.

친구(의) 책	friend's book
그분(의) 책상	his desk
이선생님(의) 사무실	Mr. Lee's office

Exercises

8 Suppose you cannot go to church this Sunday and your friend
wants to know why. Answer the question, based on the following
three reasons:

a it is snowing
b you are very busy
c you are too tired

9 Answer the question 그것은 누구의 책이에요?

a Miss Jin's
b Professor Kelly's
c Mr. Park's

10 Translate the following dialogue:

a Since I'm tired today, I am not studying.
b My business is doing well these days.
c Since I am meeting my friend today, I'm in good spirits.
d Mr. Lee is very busy these days.

11 Make up your own sentences, using the following words:

a 잘, 덕택에, 지냅니다
b 지금, 못, 집에, 바빠서, 가요
c 의, 책, 이에요, 이선생님

4 길 묻기
Asking for directions

By the end of this lesson you should be able to:
- express location and direction
- use negative sentences
- use informal verb ending -아(어/여)요
- use sentence endings -ㄹ(을) 거예요, -야 하다
- use the conjunction of condition -(으)면 (e.g., "if" or "when")
- use the postposition -(으)로

Dialogue 1 〓〓 *Mary Jin is in front of the subway station. She is looking for Seoul Railroad Station and asks a passerby for directions*

JIN: 실례합니다. 여기가 서울역입니까?
PASSERBY: 아니오, 여기는 서울역이 아닙니다. 바로 저기가 서울역입니다.
JIN: 감사합니다. 그럼, 여기는 어딥니까?
PASSERBY: 여기는 지하철역입니다.
JIN: 저쪽으로 어떻게 건너 갑니까?
PASSERBY: 왼쪽으로 돌아 곧장 가세요.
JIN: 감사합니다.
PASSERBY: 천만에요. 조심해서 건너 가세요.

JIN: *Excuse me. Is this Seoul Railroad Station?*
PASSERBY: *No, it isn't. Seoul Railroad Station is over there.*
JIN: *Thank you. What is this place?*
PASSERBY: *This is a subway station.*
JIN: *How can I cross over to the other side?*
PASSERBY: *Turn left and go straight ahead.*
JIN: *Thank you.*
PASSERBY: *You're welcome. Be careful when you cross.*

Vocabulary

실례합니다	excuse me	여기	here
서울역	Seoul Station	지하철역	subway station
감사합니다	thank you	저쪽으로	that way
아니다	not to be	돌다	turn around
저기	(over) there	천만에요	you're welcome
곧장	right away	왼쪽으로	to the left
조심하다	be cautious	건너다	cross

Language points

Expressing location and direction

Korean uses two sets of pointing words, one specifying location and the other direction. Each is relative to where the speaker and the hearer are situated.

Location
여기   here – a place near the speaker
저기   there – a place away from both the speaker and the hearer
거기   there – a place near the hearer

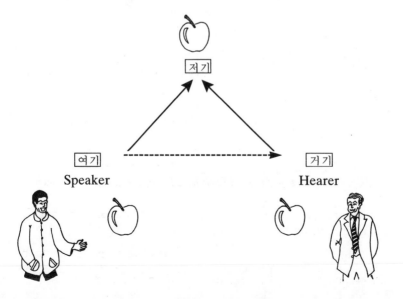

In the diagram, 여기 is used when the speaker refers to things in a place around himself or herself, while 저기 is used when the speaker refers to things in a place away from himself or herself and from the hearer. 거기 is used when the speaker refers to things in a place near the hearer (which has to be away from himself or herself.)

Direction
이리　this way – in the direction of the speaker
저리　that way – in a direction away from both the speaker and the hearer
그리　that way – in the direction in which the hearer is headed

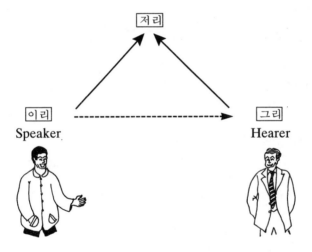

Speaker   Hearer

In the diagram, 이리 is used when the speaker specifies the direction toward which the hearer is moving or engaged in moving things, while 저리 is used when the speaker specifies a direction away from both himself or herself and the hearer. 그리 is used when the speaker specifies the direction in which the hearer is moving or engaged in moving things.

Two ways of negating Korean sentences

One way negates identification sentences, and the other negates all other types of verbs.

Negating identification sentences requires the complement to be turned into the subject to which the subject marker 가/이 is attached.

It is then followed by the negative verb 아니다, 아닙니다. This process may be summarized as follows:

Affirmative (A = B)   *Negative (A ≠ B)*
A 이/가 B 입니다   →   A 이/가 B 이/가 아닙니다

이분이 한국사람입니다.   This person is a Korean.
이분이 한국사람이 아닙니다.   This person isn't a Korean.
여기가 서울입니다.   This is Seoul.
여기가 서울이 아닙니다.   This isn't Seoul.

As we saw in Lesson 1, all other types of verbs can be negated by placing the negative marker 안 before the verb.

집에 가겠어요.   I'll go home.
집에 안 가겠어요.   I'm not going home.
김선생님은 지금 바쁘십니다.   Mr. Kim's busy right now.
김선생님은 지금 안 바쁘십니다.   Mr. Kim isn't busy right now.

More polite questions

You can use the following expressions to make questions more polite where asking for directions.

말씀 좀 묻겠습니다.   May I ask you something?
여기가 시청 앞입니까?   Is this the front of City Hall?
뭐 좀 물어봐도 될까요?   Would you mind if I asked you
                            something?

Contracted forms

You can use the following contracted forms in casual speech.

바로 여기입니다. ⎫
바로 여깁니다.   ⎬ It's right here.
바로 저기입니다. ⎫
바로 저깁니다.   ⎬ It's right there.

The consonant ㅎ

This consonant in the syllable 어떻게 is carried over to the next syllable 게 and is pronounced as 어떠케. Other examples which show this carry-over in pronunciation are 이렇게, 그렇게.

Exercises

1 You are lost on the streets of Seoul. Ask a passerby how to get to the following places:

a Lotte Hotel
b the subway station
c Chongro Street

2 Suppose you are looking at a map of downtown Seoul. Ask the friend you are with where the place you are pointing to is located on the map.

a City Hall
b Capitol Building
c post office
d East Gate Market

3 Answer the following questions according to the given cue, using one of three pointer words, outlined in Expressing location and direction above:

a 미국대사관이 어딥니까? (cue: hearer)
b 신라호텔이 어딥니까? (cue: away)
c 백화점이 어딥니까? (cue: speaker)
d 은행이 어딥니까? (cue: hearer)
e 경찰서가 어딥니까? (cue: speaker)

4 Name at least three public places where you as a traveler can do business in the city.

5 Make your own sentences, using the following words:

a 저쪽으르, 건너가다, 어떻게?
b 오른쪽, 돌다, 지하도, 건너가다
c 여기, 대사관, 아니다

6 You are giving someone who is learning Korean some grammar help. Correct his or her grammar.

a 거기가 지하철역가 입니다.
b 여기는 안서울입니다.
c 거기가 시청가 아닙니다.
d 이선생님은 지금 바쁘안세요.

7 Translate the following dialogue:

A: Excuse me. Where's there a police station around here?
B: It's right over there across the street.
A: How can I cross this street? There's so much traffic.
B: Well, you can use the underpass at the corner.
A: I see. Thanks very much.
B: You're welcome.

8 Mr. Anderson is at City Hall, but he's standing on the side opposite the Plaza Hotel (pronounced 플라자호텔), where he wants to get to. He encounters a high school student who does not speak any English. He notices an overpass to his left and heavy traffic on the wide streets. Write a realistic dialogue between Mr. Anderson and the high school student.

Culture point

On p. 56 you will find a map of Central Seoul. Look at the following: Seoul City Hall (1), Korea National Tourism Corporation (KNTC) (2), Sejong Cultural Center (3), Kyobo Building (4), U.S. Embassy (5), and Kyongbokkung (6). These are shown on the miniature map by Arabic numerals in ascending order. Located within walking distance are four major deluxe hotels: Chosun (7), Plaza (8), Lotte (9), and President (10). Major department stores, arcades, and "small or large" markets are also clustered in the downtown area, which provides foreigners with excellent shopping opportunities.

Dialogue 2 ⬚⬚ *Mr. Anderson is lost in downtown Seoul. He asks a passerby how he can get to the U.S. Embassy*

ANDERSON: 실례합니다. 길을 잃어 버렸어요. 저기가 미국대사관입니까?
PASSERBY: 아니오, 저기는 미국대사관이 아닙니다.
ANDERSON: 그럼, 미국대사관에 어떻게 갑니까?
PASSERBY: 저기 골목을 지나 가세요. 거기서 왼쪽으로 곧장 가세요.
ANDERSON: 예, 감사합니다. 여기서 멉니까?
PASSERBY: 걸어서 가면, 아마 시간이 많이 걸릴 거예요.
ANDERSON: 차로 가면 어때요?
PASSERBY: 차로 가면, 별로 안 걸려요.
ANDERSON: 아, 그래요. 그럼 택시를 타야겠어요. 아무튼 감사합니다.
PASSERBY: 천만에요.

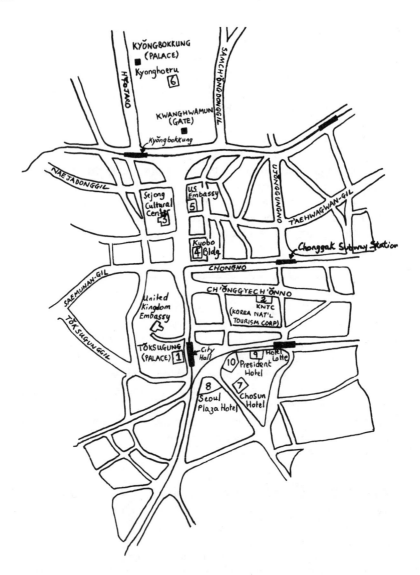

Central Seoul

ANDERSON: *Excuse me. I'm lost. Is that the U.S. Embassy?*
PASSERBY: *No, it isn't.*
ANDERSON: *Oh! How do I get there?*
PASSERBY: *Just go past the small side street over there.*
Go straight ahead from there to your left.
ANDERSON: *Thank you. Is it far from here?*
PASSERBY: *If you walk, it'll take you quite a while.*
ANDERSON: *How about by car?*
PASSERBY: *If you go by car, it won't take you long.*
ANDERSON: *Oh, I guess I'll take a taxi. Thanks anyway.*
PASSERBY: *You're welcome.*

Vocabulary

길	street	별로	particularly
잃어 버리다	to get lost	미국대사관	U.S. embassy
골목	alley	지나가다	pass by
걸리다	to take	아마	probably
걸어서	by foot	많이	much, many
멀다	far	면	if
차로	by car	택시	taxi
타다	to ride	시간	time
감사하다	to be thankful	아무튼	anyway

Language points

Informal verb ending -아(어/여)요

The informal verb ending -아(어/여)요 is used when a speaker is already acquainted with the hearer to some extent (e.g., colleagues in the office). This ending can be used to make a statement, ask a question, or give a command. Different vowels need to be inserted, depending on the nature of the vowel used in the verb stem.

Verb stem + 아/오   → 아요: 가요, 자요, 앉아요
Verb stem + 우/으/이 → 어요: 바빠요, 먹어요
Verb 하 + 여   → 해요: 일해요, 운전해요

Informal sentence ending - ㄹ / 을 거예요

When used with a verb, the informal sentence ending - ㄹ / 을 거예요 indicates some type of probability. This is an informal version of the pattern - ㄹ / 을 것이예요.

저분이 선생님일 거예요.   That man/woman is probably a teacher.

기차가 역에 도착할 거예요.   The train'll probably arrive at the station soon.

Conjunction of condition or stipulation -(으)면

The conjunction -(으)면 indicates condition (e.g., "when"), or stipulation (e.g., "if") when attached to the present stem of a verb. (In Korean the dependent clause precedes the main clause, but in English the dependent clause can precede or follow the main clause.) The form -면 is attached to the verb stem ending in a vowel or ㄹ, but the form -으면 is attached to the verb stem ending in a consonant.

시간 있으면, 전화하겠어요.   If I have time, I'll call you.

돈이 있으면, 그것을 사겠어요.   If I have money, I'll buy it.

공부를 많이 하면, 눈이 피곤해요.   When I study a lot, my eyes get tired.

There are exceptions to this rule. They are 그으면, 쉬우면, 그러면.

Sentence ending of obligation -야 하다

The obligatory sentence ending -야 하다 is equivalent to English auxiliaries such as "have to," "must," or "should." It requires different vowel insertions depending on the nature of the vowel used in the verb stem. 아, 어, and 해 are inserted respectively, after 아 / 오 vowels and 어/으/이 vowels with a consonant ending and after the 하다 verb. But no vowel is inserted after the verb stem with a vowel ending. The tense is expressed at the end of the verb.

지금 의자에 앉아야 하겠어요.   Now I'll have to sit in the chair.

저녁을 지금 먹어야 하겠어요.   I'll have to eat supper now.

도서관에서 공부를 해야 하겠어요.	I'll have to study in the library.
집에 가야 하겠어요.	I'll have to go home.
그때 집에 가야 하겠어요.	I had to go home at that time.

The postposition -(으)로

This postposition, attached to a noun, refers to the means with which someone does something or by which someone moves (by one's own volition or by vehicle, whether driving or not). There are other uses of -(으)로, which will be introduced later.

-로 (*ending in a vowel*)		-으로 (*ending in a consonant*)	
기차로	by train	무엇으로	by what
버스로	by bus		
비행기로	by plane		
배로	by ship		
고속버스로	by express bus		

Verb stem 잃

The second consonant of this verb stem becomes silent. Thus, the syllable is pronounced as 일.

Exercises

9 Assume that you are engaged in the following activities and that someone asks what you are doing. Answer the questions, using -아(어/해)요

a reading a newspaper
b playing tennis
c watching a movie
d gardening

10 Someone asks if you can take a trip to Italy. Answer the question by saying that you can do it if you have the following things:

a enough time
b a million dollars
c an airplane

11 One of your friends wants to spend time with you over the weekend. Tell him or her that you must stay at home because you have three things to do.

12 Tell a friend of yours that you will take a trip to Seoul by the following means:

a ship
b airplane
c train

13 A stranger asks you how to get to a certain place. Answer by saying he/she should go by the following:

a bus stop
b bank
c library

14 Make your own sentences, using the following words:

a 기차, 오래, 걸리다, 서울, 가다
b 극장, 오른쪽, 가다, 보이다
c 모퉁이, 지나가다, 우체국, 있다

15 A Korean friend of yours is worrying about getting caught up in the traffic during the rush hour. Explain to him what kind of public transport he should use to get around.

a taxi
b bus
c subway
d limousine

16 You are supposed to meet one of your Korean friends at the back gate of a museum, where you are supposed to go on a date. Translate the following directions. Your friend will follow these from the point when she arrives at the terminal by express bus.

a When you get off the express bus, you will see a big building straight ahead.
b When you pass it on your left, you will see another small building. It's a museum.
c Buy a ticket at the ticket booth.
d Follow the center road straight to the back gate. I will be there.

17 Suppose a foreign traveler is lost in the city and asks you for help. As the traveler has a miniature map of the vicinity, guide him/her to the City Hall, using the traveler's own map.

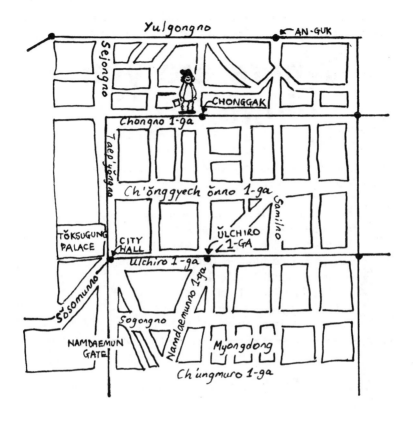

5 어디 가세요?
Where are you going?

By the end of this lesson you should be able to:
- talk about a trip you've made
- use the honorific markers 시/세
- use the postposition -에 (place and time)
- use the existential verb 있다
- use the honorific subject case marker -께서
- use the sentence ending -(이)거던요
- use the names of public places and modes of transport

Dialogue 1　◖◗　*Kim and Kang are talking about a trip to New York City*

KIM:　주말에 어디 가세요?
KANG:　주말에 뉴욕에 갑니다.
KIM:　뉴욕이 어디 있습니까?
KANG:　여기가 뉴욕입니다.
KIM:　뭐로 뉴욕에 가십니까?
KANG:　기차로 갑니다.
KIM:　언제 집에 돌아오세요?
KANG:　다음 주말에 돌아옵니다.
KIM:　그럼, 잘 다녀오세요.

KIM:　*Where are you going over the weekend?*
KANG:　*I'm going to New York City over the weekend.*
KIM:　*Where is New York City located?*
KANG:　*This is New York City (pointing to the city on the map).*
KIM:　*How (lit. By what type of transport) do you go?*
KANG:　*I go by train.*
KIM:　*When will you come back home?*

KANG: *I'll come back next weekend.*
KIM: *(Well, then,) have a nice trip.*

Vocabulary

주말	weekend	뭐로	by what
어디	where	집에	(to) home
있다	to be, exist	언제	when
뉴욕	New York City	다음	next
기차	train	잘	well
돌아오다	return	다녀오다	go and come back (honorific)

Language points

The honorific markers 시 / 세

As explained in Lesson 3, these markers are used to indicate respect on the part of the speaker to someone who is older or who has a higher position than oneself. Thus, it is not appropriate to use these honorific markers when the speaker is the subject. Examine the following pairs of sentences.

A: 어디 가십니까? Where are you going?
B: 집에 갑니다. I'm going home.

A: 어디 가십니까? Where are you going?
B: 집에 가십니다. I'm going home.

The first response is acceptable, but the second is not.

The postposition -에 *(place)*

This postposition is attached directly to a place word and is followed by 가다 "to go," 오다 "to come," or their compound verbs. It refers to a specific destination.

집에 갑니다.   (I'm) going home.
학교에 갑니다.   going to school.
도서관에 갑니다.   going to the library.
호텔에 갑니다.   going to the hotel.

The postposition -에 *(time)*

This postposition also conveys a sense of time, when a time word precedes it. It is equivalent to such English prepositions as "at," "on," "in," etc.

주말에 어디에 가세요?	Where are you going over the weekend?
월말에 집에 가요.	I'm going home at the end of the month.
오후에 도서관에 갑니다.	I'm going to the library in the afternoon.
그 사람은 정오에 와요.	He (*lit.* the man) is coming at noon.

The verb of existence 있다

The verb 있다 indicates existence, location, or possession in various contexts. Listed below are some sentences, in which the verb follows a place. In this case, the verb 있다 conveys location.

도서관은 어디에 있습니까?	Where is the library?
보스톤은 여기 있습니다.	Boston is located (over) here.
한국은 여기 있습니다.	Korea is located (over) here.

있다 should not be confused with the verb 이다 conveying equality. The verb 이다 will be discussed in the next lesson.

The pronoun 누구 *(who)*

When 누구 takes a subject case marker -가, the second syllable -구 gets dropped.

누가 공부합니까?	Who's studying?
누가 옵니까?	Who's coming?
누가 갑니까?	Who's going?

But 누구 is used with other grammatical categories such as the verb 이다 and object case markers -을/를.

이분이 누구입니까?	Who's this person?
누구를 기다리십니까?	Who are you waiting for?

Exercises

1 Choose the word which does not belong to the group:

a 비행기, 기차, 배, 자전거, 호텔
b 정오, 집, 주말, 연말, 월말
c 도서관, 뉴욕, 한국, 보스톤, 서울
d 도서관, 호텔, 교회, 집, 학교

2 Suppose you know that someone you are acquainted with is going to the following places. How would you respond to the question 그분 어디 가세요? You must use the postposition -에 in your answers.

a Seoul
b my hometown
c New York
d Boston

3 You are going to London over the weekend and one of your friends asks how you are going. Respond to the question, using the following:

a train
b express bus
c car
d taxi

4 A visitor is lost on the streets of Seoul. He asks you where the following places are located on the miniature map of downtown Seoul (see the map on page 56). Help this person out by answering his questions.

a City Hall
b subway station
c U.S. Embassy

5 Translate the following conversation:

A: Mr. Kim. Where are you going?
B: I'm going to the subway station.
A: Is someone coming?
B: Yes, my brother is visiting us. Tomorrow is my son's birthday.
A: Really? You must be excited.

6 You are giving some grammar help to someone who is learning Korean. Correct the grammar in these sentences.

a 누구은 서울역에 옵니까?
b 서울역가 저기에 있습니까?
c 뉴욕에 기차으로 가요.
d 주마레 친구 집에 가요.
e 친구가 집에 가십니다.

7 You run into your work colleague on a Seoul street. You are curious to know why he is heading towards the British Embassy. Write a realistic dialogue which might have taken place between you and your friend.

Culture point

Seoul Railroad Station (pictured opposite), constructed in 1926, is a Renaissance-style building with a huge Byzantine dome. It serves as the epicenter for Korea's land transport system, where trains travel to all the peninsula's major cities. Some 100,000 passengers enter and leave Seoul every day. In recent years, major subway lines have been connected with the station, providing passengers with easy access to downtown Seoul.

Dialogue 2 ▮▮ *Ki Soo Kang runs across Miss Kim on a Seoul street and asks her if she is expecting a visitor*

KANG: 김선생님, 어디 가세요?
KIM: 기차역에 갑니다.
KANG: 누가 옵니까?
KIM: 예, 제 아버님께서 고향에서 오십니다.
KANG: 아, 그래요? 아버님 자주 오세요?
KIM: 아니요, 가끔 오세요. 내일이 제 생일이거든요.
KANG: 아, 그래요? 언제 돌아 가십니까?
KIM: 모레 돌아 가십니다.

KANG: *Mr. Kim, where are you heading?*
KIM: *I'm heading towards the train station.*
KANG: *Who's coming?*
KIM: *My father's coming from my hometown.*
KANG: *Really? Does your father come frequently?*
KIM: *No. He seldom comes. He's coming because tomorrow is my birthday.*
KANG: *Really? When is he going back home?*
KIM: *He's going back the day after tomorrow.*

Vocabulary

아버님	father	가끔	sometimes
기차역	train station	내일	tomorrow
고향	hometown	생일	birthday
자주	frequently	모레	the day after tomorrow

Language points

Deletion of the postposition -에

The postposition -에 indicating location is generally deleted in simple sentences.

한국(에) 가요. I'm going to Korea.
학교(에) 가요. I'm going to school.
집(에) 가요. I'm going home.

However, when attached to time words, it is not subject to deletion. The following sentences without the time postposition are ungrammatical.

주말 어디에 가세요? Where are you going over the weekend?
월말 집에 가요. I'm going home at the end of the month.
연말 집에 가요. I'm going home at the end of the year.

Deletion of subject case markers

The subject case markers explained in Lesson 2 are deletable.

뉴욕 어디 있습니까? Where is the city of New York located?
여기 뉴욕입니다. This place is New York.
제 친구 옵니다. My friend is coming.

Honorific subject case marker -께서

This honorific suffix is used in place of the plain form, when an honorific noun is chosen. Using it makes one's expression even more formal and polite than simply using the honorific noun.

김선생님께서 오셨습니다.   Mr. Kim came.
김교수님께서 도서관에 가셨습니다.   Professor Kim went to the
                                       library.

어머님께서 고향에서 오십니다.   Mother is coming from
                                       my hometown.

The sentence ending -거든요

When it is placed at the end of the sentence, this ending indicates
astonishment or delight. It also indicates a minor causal condition
in a certain context, the meaning of which is used in the following:

비가 많이 왔거든요.   Because it rained a lot!
친구가 오거든요.   Because my friend's coming!
주말에 집에 가거든요.   Because I'm going home over the
                              weekend!

The postposition -에서

This postposition was introduced in Lesson 1 as a suffix indicating
the location of an event. When it precedes the verb 오다 "to come,"
it may also be used to denote the origin of an event.

어머님께서 서울에서 오셨습니다. My mother came from Seoul.
친구들이 한국에서 왔습니다.   Friends came from Korea.
편지가 고향에서 왔어요.   A letter came from my
                                       hometown.

Honorific/non-honorific verb forms and their usage

So far, we have introduced various verb forms in a rather random
fashion. We can now put these variations in perspective to present
the general principles for forming them and their relationships as
well. The following table shows the general rules for making up
the verb forms:

Types of expression	Non-honorific	Honorific
statement	stem -(아/어) 요.	stem -(으) 세요.
question	stem -(아/어) 요?	stem -(으) 세요?

request	stem -(아/어)요.	stem -(으) 세요
statement	stem -(습)니다.	stem -(으)십니다.
question	stem -(습)니까?	stem -(으)십니까?
request	NA*	stem -(으)십시오.

Rule 1 If the verb stem ends in a vowel, no additional vowel 으 is inserted between the stem and its ending for the honorific short and long forms.

Stem	*Short ending*	*Long ending*
가다	가세요	가십시오
하다	하세요	하십시오
공부하다	공부하세요	공부하십니까?
보다	보세요	보십시오

Rule 2 If the verb stem ends in a consonant, the syllable 습 is inserted between the stem and its ending for the non-honorific long forms. However, the verb stem ending in a vowel takes only the consonant ㅂ which can be used as an underneath character.

Stem	*Consonant ending*	*Stem*	*Vowel ending*
먹다	먹습니다	보다	봅니다
있다	있습니다	가다	갑니다
앉다	앉습니까?	공부하다	공부합니까?

Rule 3 The short, non-honorific ending is formed by attaching the endings -(아/어/여)요 to the respective verb stems of dark (어, 으, 이)/bright(아, 오) vowels and 하. This has already been explained in Lesson 4. However, note the following exceptions to this rule:

이다	be	이에요
아니다	not be	아니에요
바쁘다	busy	바빠요
쓰다	write	써요
기다리다	wait	기다려요
말하다	speak	말해요

Although short and long forms are both used in conversations in Modern Korean, the former is more often used in casual speech.

Rule 4 Some verb forms use the built-in honorific forms. They do not take honorific insertions -시 or -세, but yield separate lexical entries which are honorific. See page 45 for examples of these verbs.

Note: an asterisk mark (*) above and hereafter means the construction is Not Applicable (NA).

Stem	Honorific conjugations
있다	계시다, 계세요, 계십니까?
자다	주무시다, 주무세요, 주무십니다.

Exercises

8 Suppose someone you know very well is going to the following places. Respond to the question 그분 어디 가세요?, deleting the postposition -에 this time.

a church
b home
c station
d library

9 Tell your friend that you are going to the library at the following times:

a in the morning
b in the afternoon
c at noon
d in the evening

10 One of your roommates wants to know who is visiting you over the weekend. Answer, using the following:

a older brother
b father
c mother
d uncle

11 You had to miss a meeting last Monday and your supervisor wants to know why. Give your explanation, based on the following reasons:

a It snowed a lot.
b You overslept.
c Your friend came.
d I went home.

12 A group of visitors from different places came to see you to celebrate your birthday over the weekend. One of your friends wants to know where they all come from. Respond, using the following:

a New York
b Johannesburg
c Sydney
d your hometown

13 Make your own sentences, using the following words:

a 한국, 내일, 형님이, 에서, 오세요
b 제, 이거든요, 월말, 생일, 이
c 지하철, 지금, 께서, 어머님, 역, 가세요
d 지금, 가, 비, 오거든요, 많이

14 You are giving grammar help to someone who is learning Korean. Correct the grammar in these sentences:

a 주말을 친구 집에 가요.
b 아버님이 교회에 가요.
c 친구께서 식당에서 점심 먹어요.
d 편지이 서울에서 왔어요.

15 Fill in the columns for the following conjugation table:

Types of expression		Non-honorific	Honorific
statement	short form	자요	(1)
question		(2)	주무세요?
request		자요	(3)
statement	long form	(4)	주무십니다
question		잡니까?	(5)
request		NA	주무십시오

16 In front of Seoul Railroad Station you run across one of your Korean language teachers, who is curious to know why you are there at that point in time. Explain that your father has come from his hometown to visit you over the weekend.

6 이것이 무엇입니까?
What is this?

By the end of this lesson you should be able to:
- make basic requests
- respond to an identity question in the affirmative and negative
- use the additional sets of pointing words 이것, 그것, 저것
- use the topic case marker -은/는
- use the sentence endings -이에요/아니에요, -는데요

Dialogue 1  *Mr. Kim asks Ms. Jones about various objects typically found in an office*

KIM: 이것이 무엇입니까?
JONES: 그것은 책입니다.

KIM: 저것이 무엇입니까?
JONES: 저것은 책상입니다.

KIM: 이것은 책입니까?
JONES: 아니오. 그것은 책이 아닙니다.

KIM: 그것은 지도입니까?
JONES: 아니오. 이것은 지도가 아닙니다.
이것은 한국어 책입니다.

KIM: *What's this?*
JONES: *It's a book.*
KIM: *What's that?*
JONES: *That's a desk.*
KIM: *Is this a book?*
JONES: *No, it isn't a book.*
KIM: *Is that a map?*
JONES: *No, this isn't a map.*
This is a Korean language book.*

Vocabulary

이것	this thing	책상	desk
그것	that thing (away from speaker and hearer)	이다	to be
		아니다	not to be
저것	that thing (near speaker only)	한국어 책	Korean language book
무엇	what	아니오	no
책	book		

Language points

Sentence expressing an identity

The linking verb -입니다/-입니까?, as explained in Lesson 2, is a verb that identifies the predicate of a sentence with the subject.

Identity: A (이/가) B 입니다.	A is B.
이것은 무엇입니까?	What's this?
그것은 시계입니다.	It's a clock.
이것은 오늘 신문입니다.	This is today's newspaper.

The linking verb 아닙니다

The negative counterpart of the linking verb 입니다 is noun + 아닙니다. This noun normally takes the subject case marker -이/가 once the noun switches from the predicate to the subject position and assumes the function of the subject of the linking verb. Thus, in this type of negative construction, the same or a different case marker may appear twice. This is called the double subject construction.

Identity: A (이/가) B 입니다	A = B
Negation: A (이/가) B (이/가) 아닙니다	A ≠ B
이것은 연필입니다.	This is a pencil.
이것은 연필이 아닙니다.	This isn't a pencil.
저것은 공책입니다.	This is a notebook.
저것은 공책이 아닙니다.	This isn't a notebook.

More pointing words

Lesson 4 introduced two sets of pointing words such as 이리, 그리, 저리, and 여기, 거기, 저기. This section introduces two remaining sets of pointing words. The basic meaning is the same as in Lesson 4.

Thing category

이것 이	"this" + 것 "thing"	object near the speaker
그것 그	"that" + 것 "thing"	object either near the hearer or mutually understood
저것 저	"that" + 것 "thing"	object away from both the speaker and the hearer

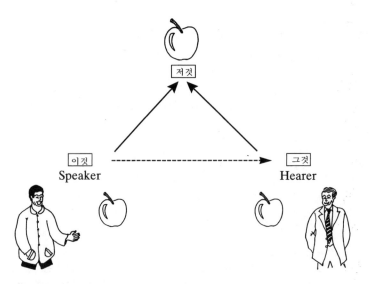

Person category

이분 this person – person near the speaker
그분 that person – person either near the hearer or mutually
            understood
저분 that person – person away from both the speaker and the
            hearer

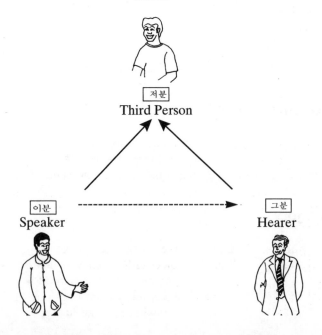

저것이 펜입니다.	That's not a pen.
그것은 연필이 아닙니다.	That's not a pencil (near the hearer).
이것은 한국어 책입니다.	This is a Korean language textbook.
이분이 김박사님이십니다.	This (person) (honorific) is Dr. Kim (with a doctoral degree).
저분은 송선생님이십니다.	That (person) (honorific) is Mr. Song.
그분은 누구십니까?	Who's that (person) (honorific)?

Note that in conversations the final consonant of all pointing words can often be dropped, as in 이거, 저거, 그거. When the subject case maker 이 follows, it may even get contracted into -게.

이것이	("this" near the speaker)	이게
그것이	("that" near the hearer)	그게
저것이	("that" away from both)	저게

The demonstrative modifiers 이, 그, 저

These modifiers can be combined with common nouns.

이 책상	this desk
이 연필	this pencil
저 볼펜	that ballpoint pen
그 학생	the student (near you)

The informal ending -이에요/아니에요

A non-honorific long ending -입니다 is often re-formed as -이에요 in an affirmative sentence and spelled this way. Women and school-children tend to adopt this form, but males prefer to use its base (original) form. When the sentence ending -이에요 comes after a noun ending in a vowel, -이 is usually contracted into -예. Also, note that the negative form of this ending is -아니에요.

그것은 책입니다.
그것은 책이에요.

이것은 책이 아니에요.
이것은 의자입니다.

이것은 의자이에요.
이것은 의자에요.
이것은 의자가 아니에요.

Exercises

1 An American student points at various objects near you and asks you what they are. Respond to his question.

a chair
b newspaper
c dictionary
d map

2 Someone asks you what the objects are that he is pointing at. Answer his questions on the basis of the pictures shown:

a 이것은 책입니까?

b 저것은 오늘 신문입니까?

c 이것은 메모지입니까?

d 이것은 연필입니까?

3 Answer the following questions, looking at the pictures shown below:

a 저분이 경찰입니까?

b 이분이 누나이에요?

c 그분이 남자입니까?
(pointing to the person on the left)

4 A toddler asks you to identify the pictures she has. Respond to her question, using -이에요.

a   b

 c

 d

Culture point

Personal relationships in a Korean office setting are vertical. They are expressed in job-related titles, ranging from the president (사장), director (전무), managing director (상무), division chief (부장), section chief (과장), assistant section chief (대리), to the new employee (신입사원). Every staff member addresses a colleague in junior rank by his or her last name with a job title. But one also addresses a senior colleague by his or her last name with a job title and the honorific suffix -님. At a workplace, a foreigner may notice that staff members low in rank are conspicuously submissive to staff members high in rank. Thus, it is not unusual for a senior staff member to request a junior staff member to provide some type of service, including requests for office supplies or objects. It is also notable that the role which a female employee assumes is usually considered minor compared with the role played by a male employee, although her higher rank can reverse this role relationship.

Dialogue 2 **CD** *Mr. Kim is looking for some office supplies and asks a junior staff member, Miss Lee, to bring one for him*

KIM: 거기에 스테플러 있어요?
LEE: 아니요. 여기 없습니다.
그것은 옆방에 있는데요.
KIM: 그럼, 클립은 있어요?
LEE: 예, 여기 있어요.
KIM: 이리 몇 개 좀 가져다 주겠어요?
LEE: 네, 그렇게 하겠습니다.
잠깐 기다리십시오.
    (*A moment later*)
LEE: 자 여기 있습니다.
KIM: 고마워요.
LEE: 천만에요.

KIM: *Is there a stapler?*
LEE: *No, it's not here.*
    It's in the next room.
KIM: *Do you have any paper clips?*
LEE: *Yes, I have some here.*
KIM: *Would you please bring several here for me?*
LEE: *Yes, I will do so (that way).*
    Just a moment, please.
      (*A moment later*)
LEE: *Here they are.*
KIM: *Thank you, Miss Lee.*
LEE: *You're quite welcome.*

Vocabulary

스테플러	stapler	좀	(polite marker)
있어요	have		
없습니다	not have	그렇게	that way or so
옆방	next room	잠깐	for a moment
자 여기 있습니다	here it is	천만에요	you're quite welcome
고맙다	to be thankful		
클립	paper clips	몇 개	some
가져다 주다	fetch		

Language points

Topic case marker -은/는

We have already studied the subject case marker -이/가, which indicates the subject of a sentence. However, when the subject is introduced as a new topic in comparison with something previously mentioned in the immediate sentences, the topic case marker -은 is attached to a subject ending in a consonant, and -는 is attached to a subject ending in a vowel. The meaning of the topic case marker is roughly equivalent to the English phrase "as for . . . ."

Consonant		*Vowel*	
창문은	window	지도는	map
분필은	chalk	의자는	chair
책은	book	지우개는	eraser

지도는 있어요.	As for a map, I have one.
지우개는 없어요.	As for an eraser, I don't have one.
책은 많이 있어요.	As for books, I have a lot.

The topic case marker can be contracted to -건, when pointing words precede it.

이것은	*이거은	이건
그것은	*그거은	그건
저것은	*저거은	저건

The verb 있습니다 (있다)

This verb is not always translated to express either location (with a place) or existence, as explained in the previous lesson. There are other English translations derived from it such as "There is/are . . ." and "Do you have . . . ?"

여기에 연필 있어요.	Here is a pen.
거기에 지우개 있어요?	Is there an eraser near you?
지우개 있어요?	Do you have an eraser with you?
옆방에 한국어 사전 있어요?	Is there a Korean language dictionary in the next room?
한국어 사전 있어요?	Do you have a Korean dictionary with you?

The opposite form of this verb is 없다, which means either "There is/are not . . . ," or "Someone does not have something."

거기에 자 있어요?	Is there a ruler (near you)?
아니오. 여기에 없어요.	No, it isn't here.
자 있어요?	Do you have a ruler with you?
아니오. 자 없어요.	No, I don't have one.

The postposition -에

This postposition expresses existence when it is used with such existential verbs as 있다, 계시다, 없다, 많다 ("to be many or much"), and 살다 ("to live"). The meaning of this postposition amounts to "at" or "in."

그분이 사무실에 계십니다.	He/She is in the office.
책상이 교실에 있습니다.	Desks are in the classroom.
책상이 교실에 없습니다.	There are no desks in the classroom.

휴게실에 사람이 많습니다.	There are lots of people in the lounge.
홍선생님 식당에 계십니다.	Mr. Hong is in the restaurant.

The sentence ending - 는데요

This ending, which is attached to the verb stem of the sentence, expresses the meaning "but," and invites some comment or request.

여기에 한국어 사전이 없는데요.	There is no Korean language dictionary here, but . . .
그분은 여기에 안 계시는데요.	He/she is not here, but . . .
사무실에 아무도 없는데요.	There is no one in the office, but . . .

Exercises

5 You have bought some office supplies such as a ruler, paper clips, a pen, and an eraser at the stationery store. Your Korean office-mate keeps asking what you have bought. Respond to these questions, using the topic case marker - 은/는.

a 자 있어요?
b 한국지도 있어요?
c 클립 있어요?
d 공책 있어요?

6 Someone asks you whether a series of objects is nearby. Respond to these questions, based on the pictures given below.

a 거기에 연필 있어요?

b 여기에 시계 있어요?

c 저기에 열쇠 있어요?

7 Imagine you are answering the phone in an office while the following personnel are out for morning break. You want to tell the caller where they are at the moment.

a Miss Lee is at the restaurant.
b Section Chief Thompson is in the lounge.
c The secretary, Miss Hong, is at the snack bar.

8 One of your senior colleagues asks whether you have the following office supplies which he can borrow, but you don't have any of them. However, you say that you don't mind looking for them. In this situation, how would you respond to his questions? For new words, refer to the English–Korean glossary at the back of the book.

a Scotch tape
b stapler
c scissors

9 Ask one of your colleagues to bring the following office supplies for you. For new words, look at the English–Korean glossary at the back of the book.

a ballpoint pen
b memo pad

c paper clips
d ink

10 Answer the following questions, according to what you have in your office or room.

a 한국 지도 있어요?
b 볼펜 있어요?
c 봉투 있어요?
d 어제 신문 있어요?

7 점심식사
Going out for lunch

By the end of this lesson you should be able to:
- read a Korean menu and order dishes
- use the past tense (plain and honorific forms)
- use the suggestive endings -ㄹ까요?/-(ㅂ)시다 (i.e., "Shall we . . . ?" /"Let's . . .")
- use the object case marker -을/를
- use the emphatic marker -도
- use the less polite informal ending -지요
- use Korean numbers (1–100)

Dialogue 1 🔲 *Mr. Kim and Miss Park talk about going out to lunch at a Korean restaurant downtown*

김: 박선생님, 점심(식사) 하셨어요?
박: 아니요. 아직 안 했습니다.
김: 그럼, 밖에서 점심 같이 하실까요?
박: 네, 그러십시다. 어디가 좋겠습니까?
김: 구내식당이 어떻겠습니까?
　　구내식당은 값이 싸고 음식이 괜찮습니다.
박: 좋습니다. 그리 갑시다.

KIM: *Miss Park, have you had lunch (meal) yet?*
PARK: *No. I haven't.*
KIM: *Well, shall we have lunch outside together?*
PARK: *Certainly. Which place would be good to go to?*
KIM: *How about going to the refectory? The refectory is cheap and the food is OK.*
PARK: *It sounds good. Let's go there.*

Vocabulary

점심하다	have lunch (plain)	구내식당	refectory
식사하다	have meals (honorific)	어떻다	(be) how
아직도	yet	값이 싸다	cheap
밖에서	outside	음식	meal
같이	together	괜찮다	OK

Language points

Past tense

The Korean past tense consists of a verb stem and an insertion
(었,았,였) between the verb stem (or plus the honorific -시 place
within the stem) and the ending.

Plain form
읽(verb stem) + 다(ending)

Honorific form
읽으 + 시(honorific) +
      다(ending)

읽 + 었 + 다

읽으시 + 었 + 다

There are three rules that change the insertion of the past tense
marker.

When the final vowel of the verb stem is -아/오, *it takes* -았

Verb stem		*Past tense*
가다	go	갔습니다
오다	come	왔습니다
보다	see	보았습니다/봤습니다
좋다	good	좋았습니다
많다	many	많았습니다

When the final vowel is any other vowel, it takes -었

Verb stem		*Past tense*
기다리다	wait	기다렸습니다
쓰다	write	썼습니다
배우다	learn	배웠습니다
가르치다	teach	가르쳤습니다
먹다	eat	먹었습니다

The verb -하다 *takes the insertion* -였

Verb stem		*Past tense*
식사하다	eat (honorific)	식사했어요 (하였어요)
공부하다	study	공부했어요 (하였어요)
좋아하다	like	좋아했어요 (하였어요)

The suggestion ending -실까요?

This ending is equivalent to English suggestion forms "Shall we . . . ?" or "Shall I . . . ?" The Korean form is obtained by adding the ending -실까요 to the verb stem.

여기 앉으실까요?	Shall we sit over here?
여기서 기다리실까요?	Shall we wait over here?
같이 도서관에 가실까요?	Shall we go to the library together?

Another suggestion ending -(ㅂ)시다

Although this ending is very similar to the one above, it is used to make a suggestion or proposal stronger. The meaning of this ending is equivalent to the English suggestion form "Let's . . ." The consonant ㅂ is added to 시다 after the verb stem ending in a vowel, but -읍시다 is taken after the verb stem ending in a consonant.

점심 밖에서 합시다.	Let's have lunch outside.
홍차 한 잔 합시다.	Let's have a cup of black tea.
의자에 앉읍시다.	Let's sit on the chair.

The object case marker -을/를

This particle, attached to a transitive verb, indicates the object case of the noun. -을 is added after a noun ending in a consonant, whereas -를 is added after a noun ending in a vowel. This object case marker is often deleted in speech.

커피(를) 하셨어요?	Did you have coffee?
텔레비젼(을) 봤어요?	Did you watch TV?
오늘 신문(을) 읽었어요?	Did you read today's newspaper?

The coordinate conjunction -고

This conjunction is used to connect two clauses or phrases and is equivalent to "and" in English. In conjoining sentences the subject of one sentence may be different from that of another, although they may share a single topic.

이 식당은 크고 좋군요.	This restaurant is big and good.
구내식당은 깨끗하고	The refectory is clean and the
음식값이 싸요.	food is cheap.
오늘은 바람이 불고 비가 와요.	Today is windy and rainy.

Exercises

1 Someone asks you what you did last weekend. Respond, basing your answers on the following activities:

a read a newspaper
b went to the movie theater
c studied Korean

2 You want to suggest to one of your colleagues that you both engage in the following activities during lunch hour. How would you do so?

a have lunch outside
b have a cup of tea
c go to the supermarket

3 Make a stronger suggestion for the activities used in 2, using the ending -(ㅂ)시다.

4 You are curious to know what Miss Lee did over the long weekend holiday. Ask her in Korean whether she did the following things, deleting the object case marker:

a went on a date
b watched TV
c traveled around

5 One of your colleagues asks you if you have had lunch yet, but you have not. Respond to his question by suggesting that you both have lunch at the following places:

a cafeteria
b Restaurant Sinra
c Damijung

6 One of your friends asks you why you have been frequenting the Restaurant Sinra lately. You want to explain that it is clean and the prices are cheap. How would you say this in Korean?

7 A few people in your office are wondering where to go for lunch. Suggest to them that the following places might be good to try out:

a refectory
b snack bar
c Korean House

8 Translate the following into Korean:

A: Have you had lunch yet?
B: No, I haven't.
A: Shall we go out to lunch together?
B: Certainly.
A: Would the refectory be a good place to go?
B: Yes. It's a big place and it's very cheap.

Culture point

A variety of Korean restaurants are scattered throughout downtown Seoul as well as other places. Most of them specialize in serving certain kinds of meals, ranging from fire-burned meats (e.g., Pulgogi and Kalbi) to Kimpap (rice and mixed ingredients rolled with green larva [edible seaweed]). A foreigner not familiar with Korean food may give it a try by dining at a restaurant which serves barbecued or wooden charcoal-grilled meats such as marinated beef and beef ribs. The prices of these menu items may seem somewhat expensive to the first-time diner, but he or she is sure to find them worth the money. It is a good idea for a group of people (or at least a party of two) to dine together at the Pulgogi House (the name of a restaurant), since many restaurants require two servings of Pulgogi and Kalbi to be ordered. While Pulgogi is being served, a bowl of rice and six or seven different side dishes may accompany it. A tip is not necessary at most restaurants, unless otherwise indicated.

Dialogue 2 ☐☐ *Mr. Kim and Miss Park enter a restaurant and order a couple of dishes. After enjoying the meal, they pay the check at the front counter*

종업원: 어서 오세요. 이리 앉으세요.
박/김: 감사합니다.
종업원: 무엇을 드시겠어요?
박: 저는 비빔밥을 하겠습니다.
      김선생님은 뭘 드시겠어요?
김: 저도 비빔밥 하지요.
박: 아주머니, 비빔밥 둘 주세요.
종업원: 네, 알았습니다.
      (*After the meal*)
김: 아주머니, 여기 계산서 주세요.
종업원: 네, 여기 있습니다.
김: 박선생님, 오늘 점심은 제가 삽니다.
박: 아닙니다. 오늘은 제 차례입니다.
김: 아닙니다. 다음에 내세요.
      오늘은 제가 내겠습니다.

WAITER: *Please come right in. Please sit over here.*
PARK/KIM: *Thanks.*
WAITER: *What would you like to have?*
PARK: *I'll have Bibimpap.*
      Mr. Kim, what would you like?
KIM: *I'll also have Bibimpap.*
PARK: *Waitress, please bring us two Bibimpap.*
WAITER: *Certainly. (Yes, sir.)*
         (*After the meal*)
KIM: *Waitress, please bring me the check (over here).*
WAITER: *Here it is.*
KIM: *Miss Park, I'm buying lunch for you today.*
PARK: *Not at all. It's my turn.*
KIM: *No, no. Please buy me lunch next time.*
      I'll treat you today.

Vocabulary

어서	quickly	차례	(one's) turn
감사합니다	thank you	내다	pay, (or in this context) treat
무엇(뭘)	what	계산서	guest check
들다	take	아주머니	waitress (married)

-도	also	사다	buy
·알다	know	둘	two
비빔밥	rice and beef with mixed vegetables and hot paste		

Language points

The topic case marker -은/는

This particle indicates an implied contrast or comparison with the information previously mentioned in a sentence. Its meaning is equivalent to the English phrase "as for . . ." Contrast the following pair of sentences.

저 비빔밥 하지요.	I'll have Pibimbap.
저는 불고기 백반 하지요.	As for me, I'll have the Pulgogi dinner.

The first sentence simply states the fact as it is. The second sentence, however, implies the covert message, "although I am not sure what you are going to order, I am going to order a Pulgogi dinner." Note that the topic case marker can replace the subject and object markers (namely -가/이, -을/를).

점심 식사(를) 하셨어요?	Have you had lunch yet?
점심 식사는 하셨어요?	As for lunch, have you had it yet?

The emphatic marker -도

This particle indicates "also" and "too," and can be attached to almost any word in a sentence. It replaces the subject and object particles.

제가 가겠습니다.	I'll go.
저도 가겠습니다.	I'll go also.
저는 불고기 백반을 하지요.	As for me, I'll have the Pulgogi dinner.
저도 불고기 백반을 하지요.	As for me, I'll have the Pulgogi dinner also.

Less polite informal ending -지요

This sentence ending is used informally in sentences of question, statement, and suggestion, which usually invite the listener's confirmation or agreement. The English equivalent for this ending is "..., isn't it?," "..., aren't you?" etc.

저는 만두국 하지요.	As for me, I'll have Wonton soup, won't I?
저 사람은 한국분이지요?	He (*lit.* that person) is a Korean, isn't he?
여기 앉으시지요.	Please sit over here, won't you?

Korean numbers (1–100)

Korean employs two kinds of cardinal numbers: native Korean and Sino-Korean numbers. The native Korean cardinal numbers (1–100) are as follows:

하나	1	열하나	11	서른	30
둘	2	열둘	12	마흔	40
셋	3	열셋	13	쉰	50
넷	4	열넷	14	예순	60
다섯	5	열다섯	15	일흔	70
여섯	6	열여섯	16	여든	80
일곱	7	열일곱	17	아흔	90
여덟	8	열여덟	18	백	100
아홉	9	열아홉	19		
열	10	스물	20		

The native Korean cardinal numbers 하나, 둘, 셋, 넷, 스물 are shortened when they are placed before a noun such as a countable noun (person or thing).

Korean numbers	Number + count (분/개)
하나	한분 one person/한개 one piece
둘	두분 two persons/두개 two pieces
셋	세분 three persons/세개 three pieces
넷	네분 four persons/네개 four pieces
스물	스무분 twenty persons/스무개 twenty pieces

The irregular verb 들다

This verb contains an honorific form and means "take" or "eat" when used in a situation where someone is eating. This final consonant -ㄹ is dropped when followed by the consonant ㅅ.

식사 많이 드세요.	Please eat a lot of food.
할머님은 식사를 많이 드십니다.	My grandmother eats a lot of food.

The contracted form 뭘

The original, full form is 무엇을 and consists of a wh- (e.g., "what") word and the object case marker. The consonant ㅅ is dropped before a vowel, resulting in the form 무얼. This form can also be further contracted to one word 뭘 in colloquial language settings.

무엇을 드시겠어요?	What would you like?
무얼 드시겠어요?	What would you like?
뭘 드시겠어요?	What would you like?

Some useful idiomatic expressions

식사 하셨어요?	Have you had a meal?
커피 하셨어요?	Had you had a coffee?
이번은 내 차례입니다.	This is my turn.
이번은 누구 차례지요?	Whose turn is it?
이번에는 내가 내겠습니다.	This time I will treat (you).

Exercises

9 Imagine you have stepped into a local Korean restaurant. A waitress dressed in a traditional Korean costume greets you and asks what dish you would like to order. Respond to her question, ordering one dish.

10 When a friend of yours has ordered a Pulgogi dinner and you want to order the same, what would you say to the waitress?

11 Answer the following questions, using the additional information supplied.

a 뭘 드시겠어요? (cold oriental noodle with hot sauce)
b 냉면 몇 그릇 (how many bowls?) 시키겠어요? (two)
c 몇 분이세요? (three)

12 When a friend of yours has ordered 비빔밥 and you want to order 갈비탕, what would you say to the waiter?

13 Yong Chul Kim, a Korean colleague in your office, has treated you to dinner many times. Now you want to treat him in return. Insist that it's your turn to take him out.

14 Respond to the following questions:

a 아침식사 하셨어요?
b 어디서 저녁식사 하시겠어요?
c 무엇을 시키겠어요?

15 Translate the following into Korean:

A: Please come right in. How many are there in your party?
B: We are a party of two.
A: What would you like to order?
B: We'll order one Pulgogi dinner and one Wonton soup.
A: Please wait a moment.

16 You are giving grammar help to someone who is learning Korean. Correct the grammar of these sentences:

a 철희씨하고 오늘 회사에 출근하지 않았다.
b 불고기 둘개 주세요.
c 식사 많이 들세요.
d Goldsmith 씨가도 김밥을 시켰어요.

17 You've got some extra money and you think that it would be a good idea to buy dinner for your girlfriend, Young Ja. How would you suggest buying dinner for her?

18 You want a waiter to bring the following dishes for you and your company. How would you order them?

a Pulgogi dinner
b rice and beef with mixed vegetables and hot paste
c Wonton soup

19 *Reading passage* Mr. Goldsmith and Miss Kim work together in an office and they very often go out to lunch nearby. One day she takes him out to a special place for lunch, but he thinks that the lunch he had wasn't so great. Try to figure out what kind of problem he had with his lunch.

어느 날 미스 김은 Goldsmith씨를 좋은 한국식당으로 데리고 갔다. 미스 김은 비빔밥을 시켰고, Goldsmith씨는 비빔냉면을 시켰다. 식당 음식은 값이 싸고 맛이 있었다. 그러나, Goldsmith씨에게는 비빔냉면은 너무 매웠다. 그래서, 다 먹지 않았다.

Key words

한국 식당	Korean restaurant	냉면	cold noodles
비빔밥	rice with mixed vegetables and hot paste	값이 싸다	cheap
		맛	taste
		맵다	hot and spicy
시키다	order	다	all of it

>차림표<

불고기 백반 Dinner with Marinated Beef	10,000원
갈비(일인분) Marinated Short Beef Ribs	13,000원
갈비탕 Short Beef Ribs Soup	5,000원
냉면 Cold Noodles with Hot Paste	5,000원
비빔밥 Rice with Mixed Vegetables and Hot Paste	5,000원

8 약속하기
Making an appointment

By the end of this lesson you should be able to:
- Make an appointment with friends
- decline an offer
- tell the time
- learn the conjunctions -는데, -지만, -ㄴ(은)후에
- learn the noun modifier -ㄴ(은)
- learn the postposition -하고

Dialogue 1 🔲🔲 *Mr. Kim and Miss Johnson work in the same office. Since Miss Johnson is learning Korean, she often takes the opportunity to try out her Korean by asking Mr. Kim lots of simple questions. One morning, she asks him what he did last night*

존슨: 어제 저녁에 무얼 하셨어요?
김: 친구 집에 갔어요.
존슨: 친구 집에서 무얼 하셨어요?
김: 텔레비젼 봤어요.
존슨: 아, 그래요?
　　　텔레비젼에서 무슨 프로그램 보셨어요?
김: 미식축구 봤는데, 아주 재미있었어요.
　　　존슨씨도 미식축구 좋아하세요?
존슨: 아니요. 저는 야구 좋아해요.
　　　미식축구는 가끔 보지만, 별로 안 좋아해요.
　　　저는 거친 운동을 싫어해요.

Vocabulary

저녁	night or evening	미식축구	American football
친구 집	friend's house	가끔	sometimes
텔레비젼	TV	별로	particularly

프로그램	program	거친 운동	violent sports
아주	very, much	싫어하다	dislike
재미있다	interesting	어제	yesterday
보다	see	야구	baseball
무얼	contraction of 무엇을 ('what')		

Language points

Types of Korean verb

There are four types of verb in Korean. These are action verbs, adjectival verbs, existential verbs, and linking verbs.

Action verbs

These indicate an action or movement performed by the grammatical subject of a sentence.

| 보다 | see | 집에서 텔레비젼 봤어요. | (I) watched TV at home. |
| 먹다 | eat | 식당에서 점심 먹었어요. | (I) had lunch in the restaurant. |

Adjectival verbs

These indicate the quality or the condition of the grammatical subject, and are equivalent to English predicate adjectives (e.g., "be good").

좋다	good	날씨가 좋아요.	The weather is good.
바쁘다	busy	김선생은 오늘 바빠요.	Mr. Kim is busy today.
많다	many/much /a lot of	저녁 시간은 많아요.	(I) have a lot of free time at night.

Existential verbs

These indicate existence, location, or possession. This kind of verb is likely to be translated into English sentences such "Something exists," "Someone or something is located in a place," "Someone has something."

있다	be/located
학생들이 복도에 있어요.	There are students in the hall.
저기에 미국대사관 건물이 있어요.	There is a U.S. Embassy building there.
없다	do not have
저는 지우개가 없어요.	I don't have an eraser.

Linking verbs

This kind of verb links a subject with its predicate, indicating equality or identification. It is often called a copula verb.

| 이다 | be | 이것은 책이다. | This is a book. |
| 아니다 | not be | 그것은 한국지도가 아닙니다. | That is not a map of Korea. |

The conjunction -는데

This conjunction is used only with an action verb and the verb 있다. Its meaning can be rendered as "and," "but," etc., depending on the context in which it is used.

어제 저녁에 텔레비젼 봤는데, 별로 재미 없었어요.
I watched TV last night, but it wasn't that interesting.

신라 식당에서 점심 먹었는데, 음식 맛이 괜찮았어요.
I had lunch in Restaurant Shinra, but the food was good.

미스리 사무실에 있는데, 만나시겠어요?
Miss Lee is in her office, and would you like to see her?

요즈음 개인 지도하는데, 아주 힘들어요.
These days I am tutoring, but it's very hard work.

The conjunction -지만

The contrastive conjuction -지만 is used with any verb to connect two clauses that stand in contrast to each other. English equivalents for the Korean conjunction -지만 are "although" and "but."

그 식당은 값이 비싸지만, 가겠어요.
That restaurant is expensive, but I'll go there (anyway).

내일은 날씨가 나쁘지만, 공원에 나가겠어요,
Tomorrow's weather will be bad, but I'll go to the park (anyway).

The noun modifier - ㄴ (은)

In Korean, the noun modifier functions in the same way as an English adjective. Noun modifiers, usually derivable from descriptive verbs, are put before the nouns they modify. In this case descriptive verbs are changed into noun modifiers by attaching the suffix - ㄴ (은) to the verb stem. Noun modifiers derived from action verbs and the verb of existence will be dealt with in Lesson 11.

싸다 cheap	싼 물건을 사겠어요.	I'll buy the cheap merchandise.
크다 big	큰 식당은 깨끗해요.	A big restaurant is clean.
좋다 good	존은 좋은 책을 샀어요.	John bought a good book.

Exercises

1 Underline the verbs in the following sentences and group them according with the four types explained earlier in the lesson.

a 제 동생은 어제 저녁에 텔레비젼을 봤어요.
b 이분이 홍선생님이십니다.
c 저 건물 뒤에 지하철역이 있어요.
d 제 친구는 돈이 많아요.

2 Someone asks you about the movie you watched on TV last night. You want to tell them that it was good, but too long. Respond, using - 는데.

3 You went to a newly opened restaurant in your neighborhood. Your friend wants to know how it was. Respond, saying that it was good, but the food was a bit expensive.

4 A colleague asks you what you did at home last night. Respond to his question, assuming that you were engaged in the activities listed below. For new words, look at the English–Korean Glossary at the back of the book.

a read a book
b watched a movie on TV
c did nothing

5 Study the following pairs of sentences which make direct contrasts. Give their Korean equivalents, using the conjuction -지만.

a I studied hard, but I don't understand the material well.
b I eat a lot, but I'm not fat.
c This merchandise is cheap, but of a good quality.

6 Fill in the blank with appropriate changes in the adjectival verbs:
a (좋다 :   ) 집은 값이 비싸요.
b 명동에는 (크다 :   ) 식당이 많아요.
c 그 가게에서는 (비싸다 :   ) 바지만 팔아요.

7 Respond to each question in Korean, based on your real activity schedule:

a 오늘 저녁에 무엇 하세요?
b 어제 저녁에 텔레비젼에서 영화 봤어요?
c 내일 저녁에 식사 약속이 있어요?

Culture point
Koreans, unlike Americans and Europeans, rarely make social or business appointments well in advance. An appointment is usually made a couple of days or some hours prior to the actual event, and foreigners accustomed to the Western appointment system may find it difficult to adapt to the Korean style. One major reason for leaving short notice lies in a desire to avoid making excuses for missing other, more important business which may surface at a later point. That is, it is potentially face-saving. For example, a junior staff member might be thrust into a situation where he has to comply with his superior's request to do some business with him, although the request conflicts with his prior engagement. Thus, many Koreans feel more comfortable responding to appointments in the order in which they are arranged.

Dialogue 2 One afternoon Mr. Kim asks Ms. Johnson if she has time to go out for dinner in a cozy restaurant downtown

김: 죤슨씨 오늘 저녁에 시간 있어요?
죤슨: 오늘 저녁에요? 오늘 저녁은 안 되겠어요.
제 친구하고 약속이 있어요.

김: 그럼, 내일 저녁은 괜찮아요?
죤슨: 내일은 좋아요.
김: 우리 저녁식사 같이 할까요?
죤슨: 좋아요. 어디가 좋겠어요?
김: 명동에 있는 한가람 식당에 가요.
죤슨: 그럼, 내일 일이 끝난 후에 5시에 전화하세요.
김: 그렇게 하겠습니다.

Vocabulary

시간	time	한가람 식당	Restaurant Hankaram
하고	with	일	work
약속	appointment	전화하다	make a phone call
저녁식사	supper	끝나다	finish (intransitive)
명동	Myongdong	내일	tomorrow

Language points

The subordinate conjunction -ㄴ(은) 후에

The temporal conjunction -ㄴ(은)후에 is used to connect two clauses. It is comared to the English expression "after something happens/has happened." -ㄴ후에 is inserted after the stem of a verb ending in a vowel, but -은후에 is inserted after one ending in a consonant.

공부를 많이 한 후에 극장에 갑시다.	After studying a lot, let's go to the cinema.
일이 끝난 후에 다방에 갑시다.	After work, let's go to the tearoom.

Note that this conjunction can be used as if it had a temporal meaning "after" or "later."

한 시간 후에 도서관에 가겠습니다.	I'll go to the library one hour later.

Echoing the question in Korean

To repeat a word or phrase uttered by another person, attach the
ending - 요 to it. This is done to ascertain what the hearer may have
heard that he or she is not sure about. Or one may need a moment
to digest what has been said.

내일 서울에 갑니까?	Do you go to Seoul tomorrow?
서울에요?	Do you mean Seoul?
한국 대통령이	Does Korea's President go to
소련에 갑니까?	Russia?
소련에요?	Do you mean Russia?
내일 저녁에	Do you have free time
시간 있어요?	tomorrow night?
내일 저녁에요?	Do you mean tomorrow night?

The verb stem - 는

This particle is attached after the stem of the verbs 있다/없다, and
identifies the location of a place.

명동에 있는 식당은	The restaurants in Myongdong
깨끗해요.	are mostly clean.
저기 있는 모자는 내 것이다.	The hat over there is mine.

Sino-Korean numbers (1–100)

Lesson 7 introduced a system of native Korean numbers. Another
system – Sino-Korean numbers (1–100) – is introduced here. They
are used when telling the time.

0	영	10	십	20	이십	30	삼십
1	일	11	십일	21	이십일	31	삼십일
2	이	12	십이	22	이십이	40	사십
3	삼	13	십삼	23	이십삼	41	사십일
4	사	14	십사	24	이십사	50	오십
5	오	15	십오	25	이십오	60	육십
6	육	16	십육	26	이십육	70	칠십
7	칠	17	십칠	27	이십칠	80	팔십
8	팔	18	십팔	28	이십팔	90	구십
9	구	19	십구	29	이십구	100	백

Reading hours and minutes

When reading the hour, native Korean numbers are used with the time counter ~시. Bear in mind that native Korean numbers 1 through 4 lose their underneath consonant when placed before the time counter.

To say "half-past" an hour, the word 반 is added right after the hourly unit.

However, when reading minutes, Sino-Korean numbers are used along with the word 분.

Another way is to read time when the long hand of the clock points anywhere between 45 and 59 minutes. In this case, the pattern __시__분전 is used. In this expression, the word 전 means "before."

지금 몇 시입니까?	What time is it now?
지금 한 시입니다.	It's one o'clock now.
지금 여섯 시 반입니다.	It's six thirty now.
지금 일곱 시 십분 전입니다.	It's ten to seven now.

The postposition -하고

This postposition is attached after a noun, and is comparable to "with" in English.

오늘 저녁에 친구하고   I'll go to the cinema with my
극장에 가요.   friend tonight.
내일은 동생하고   I'll go to the library with my
도서관에 가겠어요.   brother tomorrow.

Exercises

8 You wish to go on a date with Miss Chang, a colleague in your office, and you want to know when she will be free. Ask her whether she will be available at the following times:

a tomorrow afternoon
b tonight
c at lunchtime

9 Miss Jin, another colleague in the office, wishes to go to the movies with you after work, but you have a busy schedule lined up. What would you say to decline her offer?

10 Read the time on the clocks below:

a   b   c

11 One of your friends tries to lure you to go out to the movies tonight. You want to tell him that you can make time for him after the following events. What would you say?

a after an exam is over
b after work is done

12 You want to tell a friend to meet you at a restaurant at the following places. What would you say?

a at Myongdong
b at Chongro
c at Kwanghwamoon

13 Ask a friend to call you at home to set up your next appointment at the following times:

a 3 P.M.   b 4:15 P.M.   c 9:10 A.M.

14 One of your friends asks you if you will be free this Saturday afternoon. Tell him that you have a previous engagement with the following people at the times listed:

a with your younger brother at 10 in the morning
b with your mother at noon for lunch
c with friends in the neighborhood in the evening

15 Respond to each question, based on your real-life schedule:

a 몇 시에 주무십니까?
b 아침 몇 시에 일어나십니까?
c 점심은 몇 시에 드십니까?
d 직장에서 몇 시에 퇴근하십니까?

16 Translate the following dialogue into Korean:

A: What did you do last night?
B: I went to the movie theater with my friends.
A: Was the movie interesting?
B: Well, it was, but it was very short.

17 *Reading passage* Miss Johnson visited Mr. Lee's apartment where they watched a World Cup soccer game on TV. At that time the Korean team was competing against the Spanish team, and it ended in a draw. Although the game itself was very interesting, they didn't feel good afterwards. Try to figure out what made them feel uncomfortable at the end of the game.

Johnson씨는 어제 저녁에 친구 미스터 리 아파트에 갔다. 거기서 미스터 리하고 텔레비전에서 World Cup 축구경기를 보았다. 그 때 한국팀이 스페인팀과 시합을 하고 있었다. 그 경기는 재미있었지만, 무승부로 끝났다. 경기가 끝난 후 많은 선수들이 다쳐서, 두 사람은 기분이 별로 안 좋았다.

Key words

아파트	apartment	시합하다	compete
텔레비전	TV	경기	game, match
축구	soccer	무승부	draw
시계	watch	끝나다	finish
팀	team	다치다	get hurt

9 택시잡기
Taking a taxi

By the end of this lesson you should be able to:
- take a taxi
- communicate with a Korean driver regarding destination and direction
- pay a fare, using Korean money
- use the conjunctions -이고, -아(어)서
- use the sentence endings -ㄹ(을)수 있다, -시죠
- use the verb -걸리다
- compound verbs 내려주다 **vs.** 내려드리다

Dialogue 1 🔲🔲 *Edward Moon, a designer at the American Toy Company, is visiting Seoul on a business trip. After taking a cab at the taxi-stand in front of City Hall, he enjoys a chat with a Korean taxi driver*

운전기사: 어디까지 가세요?
손님: 동대문까지 갑니다.
운전기사: 이리 타세요.
손님: 네, 감사합니다.
운전기사: 손님은 동대문 어디까지 가십니까?
손님: 동대문 지하철역까지 갑니다.
          아저씨, 여기서 동대문까지는 멀어요?
운전기사: 그럼요. 차로 40분 정도 걸려요.
손님: 그런데, 저기 큰 건물들은 무슨 건물이에요?
운전기사: 오른쪽에 있는 건물은 교보빌딩이고,
          왼쪽에 있는 건물은 세종문화회관이에요.
손님: 아, 그래요.

Vocabulary

까지	up to	40분	40 minutes
동대문	Dongdaemoon	정도	about (roughly)
타다	get on	걸리다	take
손님	passenger	건물	building
운전기사	driver	오른쪽	right side
지하철역	subway station	교보빌딩	Building Kyobo
멀다	far	왼쪽	left side
아마(도)	probably	세종문화회관	King Sejong
아저씨	driver, uncle		Cultural Center
(운전기사)			

Language points

The particle -에서(부터)

This particle, attached to words of time or place, indicates a starting point in time, or a place from which a physical movement begins.

아침 일곱 시부터 공부합시다.	Let's study from nine o'clock in the morning.
몇 시부터 공부를 하겠어요?	From when will you study?
내일부터 아주 바쁩니다.	I'm going to be busy from tomorrow.

The particle -까지

This particle indicates "until," "up to," or "as far as," when preceded by a time expression or a place word.

어디까지 가십니까?	Up to where do you go?
남산까지 갑니다.	I go up to Mt. Namsan.
두시 반까지 집에 오세요.	Please come to my home by 2:30.

The correlational pattern -에서(부터) -까지

The above two particles can be combined to form a correlational pattern -에서(부터) -까지. Its meaning is equivalent to the English correlational phrase "from . . . to . . ."

세 시부터 다섯 시까지 회의했어요.	We had a meeting from 3 to 5.
오늘부터 내일까지 비가 와요.	It rains from today to tomorrow.
서울에서 부산까지 비행기로 한 시간 걸려요.	It takes one hour by airplane from Seoul to Pusan.

The verb -걸리다

This verb means "takes" in English, when followed by time-related nouns. This verb usually accompanies a certain mode of transportation (e.g., "by car," "by air," "by taxi," "by bus," etc.).

동대문에서 시청까지 차로 몇 시간 걸립니까?	How many hours does it take by car from Dongdaemoon to City Hall?
한 시간 걸립니다.	It takes one hour.
여기서 시청 앞까지 차로 몇 분 걸립니까?	How many minutes does it take by car from here to City Hall?
10분 정도 걸립니다.	It takes about 10 minutes.

The coordinate conjunction -이고

This conjunction is a subtype of the conjunction -고 introduced in Lesson 7. As explained earlier, it conjoins two clauses, phrases, or even sentences which illustrate a series of events. However, the conjunction -이고 is used only when the first sentence takes the linking verb -이다.

이것은 책이고, 저것은 공책이다.	This is a book and that's a notebook.
그분은 미국 사람이고, 이분은 한국 사람이다.	That's an American and this is a Korean.

The degree word 정도

This word, coming after words of time, means denotes "about," or "around" in English.

한 시간 정도 지나면 그 사람이 올 것입니다.	He will come after about an hour.
삼십 분 정도면 됩니다.	About 30 minutes will do.

Exercises

1 Suppose you take a taxi and the driver asks your destination. Tell him that you are going to the following places:

a Yongsan Subway Station
b U.S. Embassy
c Kimpo Airport

2 Suppose you take a taxi at Chongro and are heading for Dongdaemoon. You are afraid that you may not get there in time for the meeting. Ask the driver how long the journey will take.

3 One of your friends asks you how long it will take him by taxi from City Hall to the following places in Seoul. How would you respond?

a to Chongak (10 minutes)
b to Dongdaemoon Stadium (30 minutes)
c to U.S. Embassy (about 50 minutes)

4 A business acquaintance who lives in Pusan asks you how long it will take him to go from Pusan to Seoul. Tell him that it will take him different amounts of time, depending on what type of transportation he takes:

a five hours by train
b one hour by airplane
c four and half hours by express bus

5 You are pointing to one object near you and another away from you. How would you indicate the following pairs of objects in Korean?

a pen and pencil
b computer and blackboard
c desk and chair

6 While you are in a taxi you pass some modern buildings. Ask the driver what they are:

a building to your left
b building to your right
c the tall building over there

7 Translate the following dialogue between driver and passenger into Korean:

A: Where can I take you to?
B: I am going to the U.S. Embassy in Kwanghwamoon.
A: Which way should I take?
B: You drive up to City Hall and make a right turn there.
A: I see.

Culture point

Most foreigners may feel uncomfortable catching a taxi on the street in Seoul. Taxis do not always wait to pick up a customer at a taxi-stand. They may come to a rather sudden halt wherever people hail them. Understandably, some taxi drivers may refuse to pick up a customer when his direction is different from the one the taxi is heading in. However, the "Mobum Taxi" (Deluxe Taxi) (*lit*. "exemplar taxi"), which provides a luxurious service (like limousine service common in America) will pick up a customer and take him wherever he wants to go. Anyone who wants to be punctual should use the latter taxi service. Most taxi drivers, except the ones operated by the "Mobum Taxi" company, use the ride-share method and pick up one or two or more customers who are heading in the same or similar direction as the first passenger, often without his consent. Many Korean drivers, including taxi drivers, tend to smoke while driving. In this case, you, of course, have a right to ask them to refrain from smoking during driving. However, some care is needed not to lower and darken their "kibun" – see the *Culture point* of Lesson 3.

Dialogue 2 🔲🔲 *Around the time when the taxi has arrived at his destination in Dongdaemoon, Mr. Moon asks the driver to drop him off past the traffic signal near Dongdaemoon Station, where he pays the fare*

운전기사: 여기가 동대문 지하철역입니다.
　　　　　 여기서 내리시겠어요?
손님:　　　아니오. 앞으로 좀더 가세요.
　　　　　 저기 네거리에서 내려줄 수 있어요?
운전기사: 그럼, 저기 신호등 지나서 내려 드리겠습니다.
손님:　　　좋습니다.
운전기사: 자, 다 왔습니다. 여기서 내리시죠.
손님:　　　네, 그러지요. 요금이 얼마입니까?
운전기사: 6,300원입니다.
손님:　　　자, 여기 있습니다.
운전기사: 예, 감사합니다.
손님:　　　그럼, 아저씨 수고하세요.

Vocabulary

내리다	get off	지나다	go by
앞으로	forward	요금	fare
좀더	a little further	얼마	how much
네거리(사거리)	intersection	원	won
내려주다	let someone off	여기 있습니다	here it is
신호등	traffic signal	아저씨	driver
수고하세요.	goodbye	제과점	bakery

Language points

The conjunction -아/어서

This conjunction is used to connect one action to another. It expresses the close relationship between the two in addition to their temporal ordering. The conjunction is directly attached to the stem of the first verb. Verbs that take this conjunction are limited to verbs implying movement or change of posture. Some of them are 가다, 오다, 지나다, 일어나다, 앉다. However, the conjunction -고 connects two actions of other verbs, and simply expresses the notion of "after" in English.

저는 도서관에 가서 공부해요.	I go to the library and study there.
친구가 일어나서 책을 읽어요.	My friend stands up and reads a book.
저기 신호등을 지나서 내리겠어요.	I'll get off after the traffic signals there.
공부하고 잤어요.	I slept after study.

Also note that the tense is expressed in the second verb, but not in the first one.

도서관에 가서 공부합시다.	Let's go to the library and study there. (present)
도서관에 가서 공부했습니다.	I went to the library and studied there. (past)
도서관에 가서 공부하겠습니다.	I'll go to the library and study there. (future)

The auxiliary verb - ㄹ(을) 수 있다

This auxiliary verb is equivalent to "can" or "(to) be able to" in English. -ㄹ수 있다 is attached to a verb stem ending in a vowel, but -을 수 있다 is attached to a verb stem ending in a consonant. The opposite form is -ㄹ(을) 수 없다.

저기서 내릴 수 있다.	I can get off there.
거기서 잘 수 있다.	I can sleep there.
교회에 갈 수 있었다.	I could go to church.
그 책을 읽을 수 없었다.	I couldn't read the book.

Large numbers and money

Sino-Korean numbers beyond 100, together with the way these numbers are combined with various Korean monetary units, are:

100	백	1,000	천	10,000	만	100,000	십만
200	이백	2,000	이천	20,000	이만	200,000	이십만
300	삼백	3,000	삼천	30,000	삼만	300,000	삼십만
400	사백	4,000	사천	40,000	사만	1,000,000	백만
500	오백	5,000	오천	50,000	오만	10,000,000	천만
600	육백	6,000	육천	60,000	육만		
700	칠백	7,000	칠천	70,000	칠만		
800	팔백	8,000	팔천	80,000	팔만		
900	구백	9,000	구천	90,000	구만		

The basic monetary unit in Korea is 원 (won). When amounts are expressed in Arabic numerals, they are preceded by the symbol "₩." There are two kinds of units: coins and paper bills.

Coins		*Paper Bills*	
십원	(₩10)	천원	(₩1,000)
오십원	(₩50)	오천원	(₩5,000)
백원	(₩100)	만원	(₩10,000)
오백원	(₩500)		

The composite verbs 내려주다 vs. 내려드리다

The composite verb 내려주다 means "let a junior out," while 내려
드리다 means "let a senior out." So, the verb you use depends on
who it is you are letting out of the car.

역 앞에서 내려 주겠어요.	I'll let you out in front of the station. (to junior passenger)
역 앞에서 내려 드리겠습니다.	I'll let you out in front of the station. (to senior passenger)

The contracted sentence ending -시죠

This sentence ending is the contracted form of the less polite informal ending -시지요, which was introduced in Lesson 7. In casual
conversation the second syllable -지 is united with the last syllable, where the vowel 이 is dropped. This process yields the contracted form -죠.

여기서 내리시지요?	You get off here, don't you?
여기서 내리시죠?	
내일 극장에 가시지요?	You go to the theater tomorrow, don't you?
내일 극장에 가시죠?	

Exercises

8 The taxi has come near your destination and you want to get
out. Ask the driver if he can let you off in front of the following
places:

a bakery
b bank
c church

9 The taxi is approaching your destination and you want to pay
the fare. Ask the driver how much you need to pay.

10 One of your friends asks you what you are going to do tomorrow. Tell him that you have two things to do, one after the other:

a go to the library and read newspapers
b go to the bar and meet people

11 A friend asks you to do three things for her because she is sick.
·Tell her that you can do the following things:

a go shopping
b go to the bank
c clean the room

12 Someone you know asks you to lend him a large amount of
money. Tell him that you have only ₩14,000 in your pocket.

13 A friend has been to a bookstore and bought the following
three articles. Ask him how much he paid for each item.

a book
b notebook
c memo pad

14 You went to the shopping mall and bought a couple of items.
A friend of yours asks how much you paid for each item. Respond
to her question.

a hat (₩4,000)
b clothes (₩45,000)

15 Respond to each of the questions the driver asks you inside a
taxi, using the information given.

a 어디서 내려 드릴까요? (교보빌딩)
b 어디까지 가세요? (시청)
c 제과점 앞에서 내리시겠죠? (저기 신호등 지나서)

16 You know Mr. Kim very well. He is older than you and senior
to you at work. One afternoon you and he have agreed to spend
some time at Itaewon. Suggest that he takes a taxi to get there,
using the contracted informal ending -시죠.

17 Translate the following dialogue into Korean:

A: May I drop you off here?
B: No, can you go a little further?
A: I can't stop over there.
B: Then, can you let me off past that intersection?
A: Of course.
B: How much is the taxi fare?
A: It's ₩6,700.

18 Reading passage Edward Moon visited Seoul on a business trip. He took a taxi from the airport to Hotel Sinra, because he was a stranger to Seoul. But he was not very happy when he realized that it took him much longer than usual. Try to figure out what made him feel unhappy.

Edward Moon씨는 사업차 서울을 방문했다. 서울거리를 잘 몰라서 공항에서 택시를 탔다. 운전기사 아저씨는 영어를 할 수 없어서, 그는 한국말로 해야 했다. 신라호텔까지는 보통 1시간이 걸리지만, 이번에는 2시간이 걸렸다. 운전기사 아저씨가 길을 잘못 들어 시간이 더 많이 걸렸다. 그래서 택시비도 두배 많이 지불해야 했다.

Key words

사업차	on business	걸리다	take
방문하다	visit	길을	enter the
거리	street	잘못 들음	wrong way
모르다	do not know	택시비	taxi fare
공항	airport	두배	twice
운전기사	driver	지불하다	pay
신라호텔	Hotel Shinra		

10 물건사기
Shopping

By the end of this lesson you should be able to:
- do basic shopping at a Korean market
- negotiate prices
- know where you can shop in Korea
- use the long negation form -지 않다
- use base, comparative, and superlative structures
- use the contrastive conjunction -(으)나
- use the sentence endings -ㄹ(을) 것 같다, ㄴ(은/는)데요, -ㄹ(을)게요

Dialogue 1 🔲🔲 *Minsoo Lee and John Whitman have been close friends since they started working at an importing company a number of years ago. One Saturday afternoon, Minsoo suggests to John that they go shopping at a large department store*

민수: 존, 오늘 오후에 쇼핑 같이 가겠어요?
존: 좋아요. 어디로 가겠어요?
민수: 남대문 시장이 어때요?
존: 남대문 시장은 물건이 대체로 좋지 않아요.
민수: 그럼, 어디가 좋겠어요?
존: 신세계 백화점이 남대문 시장보다 더 좋을 것 같아요.
민수: 백화점은 값이 비싸지 않아요?
존: 값이 비싸지만, 질은 아주 좋아요.
민수: 그럼, 신세계 백화점으로 가요.

Vocabulary

오후	afternoon	보다 더	(better or worse) than
쇼핑	shopping	값	price
남대문 시장	Namdaemoon Market	비싸다	expensive
		질	quality

대체로	in general	-지 않다	not (long form)
물건	merchandise	백화점	department store
신세계	Sinsaekye		
백화점	Department Store		

Language points

The long negative form -지 않다

Lesson 1 introduced the short negative form of most Korean verbs, namely -안. However, another way to negate a verb is to attach the long form -지 않다 to the stem of the verb.

Stem		*Long negative ending*	
분명하다	clear	분명하지 않다	unclear
말하다	speak	말하지 않다	not speak
놀다	play	놀지 않다	not play

Although most verbs can take either form of negation, certain verbs commonly take the long form rather than the short one.

공부했습니다	studied	(X) 안 공부했습니다
		(O) 공부하지 않았습니다
서 있다	be standing	(X) 안 서 있다
		(O) 서 있지 않다

X = ungrammatical sentence, O = grammatical sentence

The particle - 만큼 *for base comparison*

This particle is attached to the noun, which is used as a base for comparison. It indicates extent, degree, or "as much as."

이 가방은 저 가방만큼 크다. This bag is as big as that bag.
내 친구는 나만큼 키가 커요. My friend is as tall as I am.

The comparison particle 보다 (더)

This particle is used to express the equivalent of English "than." When -보다 is used, the use of 더 is optional.

한국말이 영어보다 (더) 쉬워요.	The Korean language is easier (to learn) than English.
기차는 차보다 (더) 빨라요.	The train runs faster than the car.

The superlative word of an adjectival verb

In order to indicate the greatest degree when three or more items are compared, adjectival verbs in Korean can take the superlative words (제일, 가장).

이것이 제일(가장) 비싸요.	This thing is the most expensive.
롯데백화점이 가장 좋아요.	Lotte Department Store is the best.

The sentence ending -ㄹ(을) 것 같다

This sentence ending is used with any type of verb and indicates the likehood of a certain event. Its meaning is equivalent to the English expression "is likely to be," "might do . . .". -ㄹ 것같다 is inserted after a stem ending in a vowel, but -을 것같다 is inserted if the stem ends in a consonant.

이것이 비쌀 것 같다.	This thing seems to be expensive.
그 학생이 책을 읽을 것 같다.	The student seems to be reading a book.
여기가 시청일 것이다.	This place seems to be City Hall.

The adjectival verb 어떻다

This verb literally means "to be (some way)," "to be (what way)," or "to be (how)." English translations of this verb may vary, depending upon the context used. It is irregular in the past, present, and future tenses.

Stem	Present	Past	Future
어떻다 be (how)	어때요	어땠어요	어떻겠어요

오늘 날씨는 어때요?	How is today's weather?
소풍은 어땠어요?	How was your picnic?
내일 미도파 백화점이 어떻겠어요?	How about (going to) Midopa Department Store tomorrow?

Exercises

1 A saleswoman at a general store keeps asking you whether you want to buy the following item. Tell her you are not interested in buying them, using the long negative form. Look in the Glossary for new words.

a towel
b jeans
c short pants

2 Look at the pictures and compare two objects, using the base comparison form - 만큼:

  a   b

3 Look at the pictures and compare two objects, using the comparative comparison form - 보다(더):

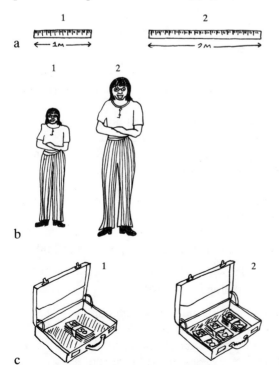

4 Look at the pictures and answer these questions:

a 어느 사람이 가장 뚱뚱해요?

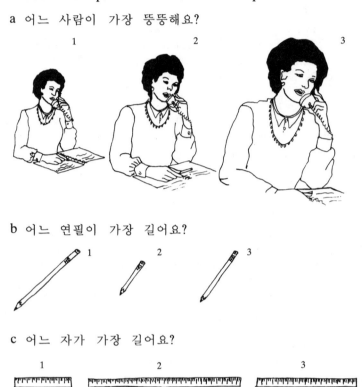

b 어느 연필이 가장 길어요?

c 어느 자가 가장 길어요?

5 At a general goods store you have looked at a number of items. Although they are good-quality merchandise, you are not interested in buying them because they look expensive. Tell a salesman that the following items look expensive:

a necktie
b shoes
c T-shirt

6 Suggest to a friend of yours that he go shopping at the Midopa Department Store.

7 Translate the following dialogue into Korean:

A: Would you go shopping with me this afternoon?
B: I'm a little bit busy this afternoon.
A: Well then, how about tomorrow?
B: I am free tomorrow.
A: Call me after work tomorrow.

Culture point

Price haggling is a well-known phenomenon at most Korean stores such as those in Itaewon, one of the busiest shopping districts in Seoul, which is frequented by foreigners. Although it is difficult to see the rationale behind this practice, many Korean shopkeepers customarily make the customer feel good by giving them a discount for the merchandise they purchase! However, don't feel too pleased about the discount because in most cases Korean merchants may have already raised the price of the merchandise by the same margin. Shoppers may end up paying the right price for the merchandise after the discount has been given. It is also possible that they may be left to pay more than the original price should it be raised by more than the amount of the discount. However, foreigners who shop at department stores may not get a discount, and should assume all merchandise is to be sold for the marked price. It is usually a good idea to shop at department stores at a certain time of the year when they set out bigger bargains for a sales promotion.

Dialogue 2 🔲 *Mr. Lee and Mr. Whitman arrive at the General Goods Store in Dongdaemoon and go into the luggage section. A saleswoman welcomes them with a beaming smile*

점원: 어서 오세요. 뭐 찾으세요?
민수: 짐가방 좀 볼 수 있어요?
점원: 보세요. 빨간 것, 파란 것, 노란 것 여러 가지가 있어요.
존: 이 빨간 가방은 얼마예요?
점원: 이만 오천 원입니다.
　　　그 가방은 값은 싸나, 디자인이 안좋아요.
민수: 이 노란 가방은 어때요?
점원: 그 가방은 튼튼해서 값이 비싸요.
　　　오만 사천 원입니다.
민수: 너무 비싼데요. 좀 깎을 수 없어요?
점원: 가만있자. 그럼, 깎아서 사만 원만 내세요.
민수: 아가씨, 크레디트카드 받으세요?
점원: 물론 받지요.
존: 제 것도 깎아 주세요. 저는 현금으로 낼게요.
점원: 네, 좋습니다. 삼만 원만 내세요.
존/민수: 감사합니다.

Vocabulary

어서	quickly	너무	too much
찾다	look for	내다	pay
짐가방	luggage bag	크레디트카드	credit card
빨간(것)	red (thing)	받다	accept
파란(것)	blue (thing)	현금	cash
노란(것)	yellow (thing)	물론	of course
여러 가지	many kinds	깎다	cut down
값이 싸다	cheap	가만있자	let me see
디자인	design	점원	salesperson
튼튼하다	sturdy		

Language points

The ㅎ irregular verbs

The stem of certain verbs drops ㅎ when it modifies to a following noun.

빨갛다	red	파란 것	blue/green thing
빨간 가방	red bag	노랗다	yellow
빨간 것	red thing	노란 가방	yellow bag
파랗다	blue/green	노란 것	yellow thing
파란 가방	blue/green bag		

When it has been mentioned in the previous sentences, in the above color-modified words, 가방 can be replaced with the pronoun 것.

The contrastive conjunction -(으)나

The contrastive ending -지만 ("although," "but") was introduced in Lesson 8. Here is another ending of the same kind which is somewhat less colloquial than -지만. It connects two clauses which contain contrasting values. -나 is used after a verb stem which ends in a vowel, while -으나 is used after a verb stem ending in a consonant.

이 물건은 좋으나 사지 않겠어요.	Although this merchandise is good, I won't buy it.
지금 바쁘나 김선생을 만나겠어요.	Although I'm busy, I'll meet Mr. Kim.

The exclamatory ending - ㄴ(은/는)데요

This sentence ending is used to indicate interest, surprise, delight, and other emotions shown by both the speaker and the hearer. The ending - ㄴ(은)데요 is attached to adjectival verbs and to the verb of identification 이다, while the ending -는데요 is used in other verbs.

싸다	cheap	이 책은 값이 싼데요.	This book is cheap!
작다	small	이 교실은 작은데요.	This classroom is small!
이다	be	이것은 한국어책인데요.	This is a Korean book!
가다	go	내 동생이 거기에 가는데요.	My younger brother goes there!

The particle 만

This particle can be attached to almost any word in a sentence. It expresses exclusivity and is equivalent to "only."

그 책만 주세요. — Give (me) only that book.
동물원은 오늘만 문을 닫아요. — The zoo closes only today.

The sentence ending - ㄹ(을)게요

This ending, when attached to the stem of any action verb and the verb 있다, expresses the speaker's intention in a casual conversation.

오늘 저녁은 제가 낼게요. — I'll treat you tonight.
저는 냉면을 먹을게요. — I'll have cold noodles with hot paste.
이 가방은 현금으로 지불할게요. — I'll pay for this bag in cash.

Exercises

8 You are at a luggage store and want to have a look at four bags of different colors. Ask the storekeeper how much each bag is:

a yellow bag
b red bag
c blue bag

9 You are at a clothing store and you want to have a look at a couple of shirts. Ask the storekeeper whether you can do so:

a blue T-shirt
b red T-shirt
c yellow T-shirt

10 You think that the price of a T-shirt sounds too much, and you want to barter the price down. Ask the salesman whether he can give you a discount on it.

11 You want to buy the sturdy-looking piece of luggage which the sales assistant has brought out for you. Tell him that you won't buy it (because it is expensive), although it is a good luggage bag.

12 You think that the price of the following merchandise is too high. Tell the saleswoman that it is too expensive, using the informal sentence ending -데요.

a purse
b pair of socks
c red hat

13 The store owner puts out a T-shirt, a pair of socks, and a blue bag. Tell him that you want to buy only the blue bag.

14 You want to buy a pretty hat at the store and pay for it. Tell the salesman that you want to pay in cash. Use the casual sentence ending -께요.

15 You are helping someone who is learning Korean with their grammar. Correct these sentences:

a John은 요즈음 도서관에서 안 공부한다.
b 저기가 있는 반바지 주시겠어요?
c 빨갛은 바지 사겠어요.
d 저 푸른 가방은 어떻애요?

16 Translate the following dialogue into Korean.

A: May I look at some school bags?
B: Certainly. Which color would you like?
A: I'd like white, please.
B: These are white ones. These bags look nice and durable.
A: How much is this brown bag?
B: It's ₩45,000. But I'll give you a big discount since you are a student.
A: Thanks very much.

17 Respond to each question:

a 요즈음 어느 백화점에 자주 가십니까?
b 지금 무슨 색 양말을 신고 있습니까?
c 구두는 무슨 색깔입니까?

18 Reading passage Min Soo Lee and John Whitman went to the discount store at Itaewon in Seoul. Min Soo bought some pairs of white socks at one store, while John bought the same kind of socks at the other store. They were very surprised when they realized that they bought the same things at different prices. Try to figure out who got the better price. Who couldn't buy anything, and why?

민수는 어제 오후에 John과 함께 이태원에 있는 한국 가게에 갔다. 민수는 어느 한 가게에서 양말 두 켤레에 5,000원 주고 샀으나, John은 값을 깎아서 4,000원에 샀다. 그 가게의 물건 값이 비싸서 민수는 빨간 시계를 살 수 없었다. John은 파란 넥타이를 샀는데, 값을 깎아서 12,000원에 현금으로 샀다.

Key words

오후	afternoon	물건	merchandise
이태원	Itaewon	비싸다	expensive
한국 가게	Korean store	빨간	red
양말	socks	넥타이	necktie
켤레	pair	현금	cash
값을 깎다	cut the price		

·11 주말여행
Weekend trip

By the end of this lesson you should be able to:
- talk about a trip to Korean cities
- make a ticket reservation
- use the sentence endings -ㄹ(을)까 하다, -(으)면 됩니다
- use the conjunctive proposition -하고
- use the relative clause marker -ㄴ(은)/는/ㄹ(을)
- use the progressive tense form -고 있다
- use the conjunctive postposition -하고
- use the days of the week
- use the particle (-이)나

Dialogue 1 *Jane Smith is a freelance writer on the Seoul Press where Thomas Moon, a Korean-American, works as editorial assistant. One Friday afternoon she runs across him by the office elevator*

문: 이번 토요일하고 일요일에 무얼 하세요?
제인: 글쎄요. 설악산에 갈까 합니다.
문: 아, 그러세요. 무엇으로 가세요?
제인: 비행기나 기차로 갈까 해요.
문: 기차가 더 편하고 안전할거예요. 언제 떠나세요?
제인: 토요일 새벽 6시 30분에 떠날까 해요.
문: 기차로 여기에서 설악산까지 얼마나 걸리지요?
제인: 약 3시간 걸리지요.
문: 갔다가 언제 오세요?
제인: 일요일 저녁에 늦게 돌아올까 해요.
문: 그럼, 잘 다녀 오세요.

Vocabulary

이번에	this time	새벽	at dawn
토요일	Saturday	늦게	late
일요일	Sunday	돌아오다	return
설악산	Mount Sorak	다녀오다	go and come back (honorific)
비행기	airplane		
기차	train	천만에요	you're (quite) welcome
편하다	comfortable		
안전하다	safe	글쎄요	let me see
떠나다	leave	무엇으로	by what

Language points

The sentence ending - ㄹ(을)까 하다

This ending is used to indicate a speaker's tentative plans about something. It is always used with action and 있다 verbs. -ㄹ까하다 is used after a vowel, but -을까하다 is used after a consonant.

일요일에 시내구경을 나갈까 합니다. — I'm planning on touring around downtown on Sunday.

내일 오후에는 극장에 갈까 해요. — I'm planning on going to the theater tomorrow afternoon.

The particle -(이)나

This particle, when attached to a noun, indicates a selection or option. It is equivalent to "or."

부산이나 경주에 가겠어요. I'll go to either Pusan or Kyongju.

연필이나 펜을 빌려 주세요. Please lend me either a pencil or a pen.

The conjunctive postposition -하고

This conjunction is used to connect two or more nouns, and is equivalent to "and." It is attached to the first noun.

오늘하고 내일은 비가 올겁니다.	Today and tomorrow it rains.
교실에 책상하고 의자가 많이 있어요.	There are many desks and chairs in the classroom.

The compound verb 갔다 오다

This verb phrase literally means "going to a certain place and coming back from there," and is equivalent to "have been to," or "have come back from." Note that the tense is reflected in the second element 오다.

어디 갔다 오세요?	Where've you been?
학교에 갔다 옵니다.	I've been to school.
롯데백화점에 갔다 왔어요.	I've been to Lotte Department Store.

Days of the week

월요일	Monday	금요일	Friday
화요일	Tuesday	토요일	Saturday
수요일	Wednesday	일요일	Sunday
목요일	Thursday		

오늘은 무슨 요일입니까?	What day (of the week) is it today?
수요일입니다.	It's Wednesday.

Exercises

1 A friend of yours asks you what you are going to do over the long holiday weekend. Tell him that you are considering doing these things:

a sightseeing in downtown Seoul
b going to Chejudo by air
c going swimming

2 You are standing at the bus stop and someone asks which bus goes to Itaewon. Tell him that either #35 or #56 goes there.

3 Circle the correct particle:

a 연필(이나, 나) 책을 사겠어요.
b 신세계 백화점(이나, 나) 미도파 백화점에 가겠어요.
c 시장에서 모자(이나, 나) 구두를 사겠어요.

4 You are giving an American who has recently joined your company some bus scheduling information. Tell her that two buses go to the following places:

a #23 and #45 (City Hall)
b #46 and #67 (U.S. Embassy)

5 You are at the train station and a passenger asks you which train goes to Pusan. Tell him that the trains indicated below will probably go there at the following times:

a 새마을호 at 10:30 A.M.
b 무궁화호 at 3:35 P.M.

6 You run across a friend of yours on Broad Street in downtown Seoul, and she asks you where you have been. Tell her that you have been to the Midopa Department Store.

7 Translate the following dialogue into Korean:

A: What are you going to do this weekend?
B: Let me see. Maybe I will go to Chejudo by air.
A: Are you going to meet someone there?
B: Well, my uncle lives there.
A: Oh, I see. Have a good trip.
B: Yeah, I will.

8 Fill in the blanks in this dialogue:

A: 어디 갔다 오세요?
B:
A: 거기서 무얼 샀어요?
B:
A: 거기 물건 값은 어땠어요?
B:
A: 나도 다음에 시간 나면, 거기 가야겠어요.
B:

Culture point

Mount Sorak is a popular tourist resort which a foreign traveler should not miss visiting. This mountain is famous for its steep peaks of granite, cut sharp by nature, and for the beautiful valleys beneath it. Its multicolored maple foliage in the autumn season attracts an especially large number of not only domestic, but also foreign, tourists. Designated as part of the Mount Sorak National Park by the Korean government, it includes first-rate hotels, inns, convenience stores, parking lots, and other public facilties, including camp sites. A cable car 3,610 foot (1,100 meters) long connects the Park entrance to the top of the mountain. Other points of interest in the outer area of Mount Sorak are Pisondae Plateau, from which an angel is said to have ascended to heaven, and Osaek mineral water, which many Koreans drink, hoping to be relieved of digestive ailments. Tourists can use various means of transportation to get to this resort area. From Seoul, it takes about one hour by air and four hours by train to get to Mount Sorak.

Dialogue 2 **⚇** *The next morning Jane Smith gets to the station and buys a ticket to Mount Sorak*

제인: 실례합니다. 기차표를 어디서 팔아요?
여행객: 저기 매표구에서 팝니다.
제인: 감사합니다.
(Jane approaches the ticket window)
제인: 설악산행 표 한 장 주세요.
매표원: 여기 있습니다. 설악산 가는 기차는 두시에 있어요.
제인: 설악산행 열차는 몇번 플랫 홈에서 출발합니까?
매표원: 6번 홈에서 떠납니다. 1시 45분까지 타셔야 합니다.
제인: 예, 잘 알았습니다.
매표원: 지금 6번 홈에 열차가 들어오고 있는데요.
　　　 그 열차에 타시면 됩니다.

Vocabulary

실례합니다	excuse me	장	counting unit for tickets
기차표	train ticket		
팔다	sell	열차	train
매표구	ticket booth	(플랫트) 홈	platform

설악산행	bound for	출발하다, 떠나다	leave
	Mt. Sorak	잘 알았습니다	understood well
표	ticket	들어오다	enter

Language points

The dependent noun - 행

This noun is attached to the traveler's destination. The English equivalent of this is "bound for a certain place."

부산행 기차표	ticket to Pusan
서울행 기차표	ticket to Seoul
미국행 비행기표	ticket to America

The noun counter - 장

This counter, when attached to numerals, is used to count paper or tickets of any type. It is equivalent to the English expression "a piece of." The combination of the numeral and the counter must follow the thing(s) being counted.

종이 한 장	two pieces of paper
열차표 세 장	thirteen train tickets
비행기표 두 장	two airline tickets

The relative clause marker - ㄴ(은)/는/ㄹ(을)

We have introduced the noun modifier - ㄴ (은), used with adjectival verbs, in Lesson 8. This indicates a quality, quantity, or the extent of the noun modified. This modifier, however, can also be used to relativize the adjectival verb of a sentence to the main sentence.

집이 좋다	the house is good	집이 좋은 사람	the person who has a good house
키가 크다	tall	키가 큰 사람	the person who is tall

When the relative clause marker is attached to the stem of the action verb, it indicates the *past tense*:

지나갔다 passed	+	버스 bus	→	지나간 버스 the bus which passed
도서관에서 공부했다 studied at the library	+	학생 student	→	도서관에서 공부한 학생 the student who studied at the library
책을 읽었다 read the book	+	학생 student	→	책을 읽은 학생 the student who read the book

But when the action verb is relativized, the relative clause marker -는 is taken to indicate the *present tense*:

지나가다 pass	+	버스 bus	→	지나가는 버스 the bus that passes
도서관에서 공부하다 study at the library	+	학생 student	→	도서관에서 공부하는 학생 the student who studies at the library
책을 읽다 read the book	+	학생 student	→	책을 읽는 학생 the student who reads the book

To indicate the *future tense* the relative clause marker -ㄹ(을) is used with action verbs as well as with adjectival verbs.

지나가다 pass	+	버스 bus	→	지나갈 버스 the bus which will pass
도서관에서 공부하다 study at the library	+	학생 student	→	도서관에서 공부할 학생 the student who will study at the library

The progressive tense form -고 있다

This ending, preceded by action verbs, expresses the notion of continuing an action or process. Here again, the tense is reflected in the second element.

학생들이 지금 도서관에서 공부하고 있어요.	Students are now studying at the library.

학생들이 그 때 도서관에서 공부하고 있었어요.	Students were then studying at the library.
지금 기차가 역에 들어 오고 있어요.	Right now, the train is entering the station.
버스가 정류장에 들어 오고 있었어요.	The bus was entering the station.

The sentence ending -(으)면 됩니다

This ending, when used with any type of verb, expresses a speaker's suggestion for a hearer to engage in some appropriate action in a given situation. The English equivalent of it is "All you have to do is . . .".

지금 열차에 타시면 됩니다.	You only have to get on the train.
저를 따라 오시면 됩니다.	You only have to follow me.
그 책을 읽으시면 됩니다.	You only have to read the book.

Exercises

9 Assume you need to buy three tickets bound for the following places. Ask a clerk at the ticket booth to issue them for you.

a one ticket for Pusan
b two tickets for Kyongju
c three tickets for Kwangju

10 At the crowded station you need to get a train ticket bound for Mount Sorak. Ask a passerby where you can get one.

11 Ask the clerk at the ticket booth to give you just one ticket for Pusan.

12 You notice that a train is just arriving at platform #6. Ask people around you whether the train will go to Pusan.

13 Someone calls you at home and asks what you are doing. Tell him that you are doing the following:

a reading today's newspaper
b talking with friends
c doing nothing

14 A passenger hurries into the station and asks around to find which train goes to Kyoungju. You are sure that train #101 on platform #7 is about to leave for Kyoungju. Tell him all he needs to do is to get on that train.

15 You are helping someone who is learning Korean. Correct the following grammar:

a 지금 들어 왔은 기차가 부산에 갑니다.
b 도서관에서 잡지를 읽근 학생들은 공부를 잘한다.
c 기차를 타은 손님들은 미국 사람들이다.

16 Rearrange these words to make meaningful sentences:

a 있어요, 미국에, 비행기, 가는, 10시에
b 부산, 있어요?, 고속버스, 몇 시에, 가는
c 지하철, 수원행, 있어요, 세 시에

17 You are on a local train bound for Pusan and a Korean passenger sitting nearby asks you a number of questions. See how many questions you can answer:

A: 어디까지 가세요?
B:
A: 어느 역에서 타셨어요?
B:
A: 이 기차는 몇 시에 부산에 도착합니까?
B:

18 Translate the following dialogue into Korean:

A: What are you going to do over this weekend?
B: I will probably go to New York City.
A: How do you get to New York City?
B: By car.
A: When are you planning to return?
B: I will return by late Sunday night.

19 Reading passage ⟦▢▢⟧ Thomas Moon took a train to Kwangju, where one of his brothers lives. Although it took him some hours to get there, the trip wasn't too uncomfortable. After

getting off the train, he took a bus and went to his brother's house.
In reading the passage, try to figure out how many hours it took
him to get to his destination by train and what number bus he took
at the railroad station to get to his brother's house.

톰은 지난 주말에 남쪽에 있는 광주에 기차를 타고 갔다. 서울
역에서 기차를 타고 대전을 지나서 광주에 갔다. 서울에서 광주
까지는 4시간 걸렸다. 기차 안에는 승객이 많았지만, 불편하지는
않았다. 광주역에 도착해 차에서 내려 버스 정류장으로 갔다. 거
기서 7번 버스를 타고 송정리에 있는 형님 집으로 갔다.

Key words

주말	weekend	승객	passengers
남쪽	south	불편하다	uncomfortable
광주	Kwangju city	내리다	get off
역	station	정류장	station (bus stop)
대전	Taejon city	송정리	(the town of) Songjonglee
지나다	go by	형님	one's older brother
걸리다	take		

12 은행에서
In the bank

By the end of this lesson you should be able to:
• open a bank account
• withdraw cash
• fill out a withdrawal slip
• use the conjunction -(으)니까
• read dates, months, and years on a calendar
• use the phrasal endings -(으)러, -(으)려고, -(으)려면
• use the conjunctive particle -와/과
• use the sentence ending -이 필요하다

Dialogue 1 🔲🔲 *James Park, an intern at a major Korean stock exchange company, wants to open a general account at a Korean bank nearby. A bank teller instructs him what to do*

행원: 어떻게 오셨어요?
박: 예금을 하려고 왔어요.
행원: 무슨 예금으로 하시겠어요?
박: 보통예금으로 하겠어요.
행원: 우선 이 표에 성함과 주소를 기입하세요.
      비밀번호와 날짜도 적으셔야해요.
박: 저는 도장이 없으니까 서명을 하겠어요.
행원: 그럼, 도장칸에 서명을 하세요.
박: 예, 잘 알았습니다.
      (한참후에)
박: 다 기입했습니다.
행원: 저기 소파에 앉아서 잠깐만 기다려 주세요.
박: 그렇게 하지요.
행원: 손님, 통장 여기 있습니다.
박: 예, 감사합니다. 수고하세요.
행원: 안녕히 가세요.

Vocabulary

예금	savings	비밀번호	PIN number
예금하다	deposit (verb)	날짜	date
보통예금	general (bank) account	적다	write
		도장	wooden stamp
우선	first of all	칸	column
표	slip	서명	signature
성함	name (honorific)	소파	sofa
주소	address	잠깐만	for a moment
기입하다	fill in	통장	passbook

Language points

The purpose ending -(으)려고

This ending is used with any action verb and indicates the purpose of the subject. The English equivalent of this phrase is "in order to." The suffix 으 is inserted after the verb stem ending in any consonant (apart from ㄹ).

이 선물을 동생에게 주려고 샀습니다.	I bought this gift for my younger brother/sister.
예금을 하려고 은행에 갔습니다.	I went to the bank to make a deposit.
차를 사려고 돈을 빌렸어요.	I borrowed money to buy a car.

The conjunctive particle -와/과

This particle is interchangeable with -하고, explained in Lesson 11, although the former is more widely used in written Korean.

교실에 책상과 의자가 많이 있어요.	There are many desks and chairs in the classroom.
John은 미도파 백화점에서 모자와 구두를 샀다.	John bought a hat and shoes at the Midopa department store.

The causal conjunction -(으)니까

This conjunction is used with all verbs and indicates the cause and effect relationship between the first and second clauses in a sentence. The English equivalent is "because," "as," "since." Although this conjunction is interchangeable, as explained in Lesson 3, the conjunction -(으)니까 differs from the conjunction -어(아/여)서 in that the latter pattern cannot be used when the second clause involves some type of request.

눈이 오니까,
　방으로 들어 갑시다.

Since it's snowing, let's go into the room.

텔레비젼이 재미 없으니까,
　보지 않았어요.

Since TV wasn't interesting, I didn't watch.

(X) 아기가 방에서 자서,
　조용히 합시다.

Since the baby is sleeping, let's be quiet.

Months of the year

Sino-Korean number words are used for the months of the year. Another word, 월, is used to indicate "month."

일월	January	칠월	July
이월	February	팔월	August
삼월	March	구월	September
사월	April	*시월	October
오월	May	십일월	November
*유월	June	십이월	December

Days of the month

The reading of days of the month consists of Sino-Korean number words and another word, 일, to indicate "day."

4월 20일　(April 20th)
6월 14일　(June 14th)
8월 29일　(August 29th)

Years

For days of the year, Sino-Korean number words are used. Another word, 년, is used to indicate "year."

Note: An asterisk (*) indicates the irregular Sino-Korean numbers 6 and 10.

1990년 3월 12일	March 12, 1990
1994년 6월 13일	June 13, 1994
오늘은 몇 일입니까?	What day of the month (date) is it today?
1994년 6월 13일입니다.	It's June 13, 1994.

Exercises

1 You have bought a couple of gifts for your family at the Midopa Department Store. A friend of yours asks you who you bought them for. Respond to his question:

a a pair of socks for your younger sister
b ballpoint pen for your uncle
c T-shirt for your grandmother

2 You happen to meet someone you know well at the local bookstore, and she asks what you bought there. Tell her that you bought a dictionary and a pen.

3 You missed the staff meeting at the place you work, and your supervisor asks you why you did not attend the meeting. Tell him that, since you were sick, you couldn't get to the meeting.

4 You quit reading the book you bought a few days ago, and a friend of yours, who happened to know about this, asks you why. Tell her that, since it was no fun, you gave up reading the book.

5 You have come out in the middle of a show at the movies, and the man at the entrance asks you why you did not stay till the end. Tell him that, since it was no fun, you came out in the middle.

6 A child visiting your home starts shouting while a baby is fast asleep nearby. Ask him to be quiet, since the baby is sleeping.

7 Answer each question, based on real life:

a 언제 태어났어요?
b 오늘은 몇 일입니까?
c 어제는 몇 일이었습니까?

8 Look at the following calendar, marked with various events happening in May:

월	화	수	목		금	토	일
	1	2	3		4	5	6 (gym)
7	8	9	10		11	12	13
14	15 (movie)	16	17		18	19	20 (picnic)
21	22	23	24		25	26	27
28	29	30	31 (dance party)				

a 몇 일에 체육관에 갑니까?
b 몇 일에 영화관에 갑니까?
c 댄스파티에는 무슨요일에 갑니까?

9 You are at the bank and a teller asks what she can help you with. Tell her that you want to open a savings account.

10 Translate the following dialogue into Korean:

A: What can I help you with?
B: I came here to open a savings account.
A: Just fill out the form there.
B: All right.

11 Complete the following dialogue:

A: 무슨 예금 하시겠어요?
B:
A: 도장 있어요?
B: 아니요, 저는 미국인이니까, 도장이 없어요.
A:
B: 예, 다했습니다.
A:
B: 예, 알겠습니다.

Culture point

The unit of Korean currency is the won (w). There are 1, 5, 10, 50, 100, and 500 coins, while paper bills come in the following amounts: 1,000, 5,000, and 10,000. Koreans do not use checks, as Americans and Europeans do: instead, they use cash in their daily transactions. When they need to carry a large amount of cash for some business transaction or other, they have to convert cash into bank-certified checks whose minimum unit is ₩100,000. A foreign traveler can have foreign currency or traveler's checks cashed into Korean won at the foreign currency booth of any authorized bank, including foreign exchange banks. He or she can use several Korean branches of American banks in downtown Seoul. The exchange rate fluctuates on a daily basis, but is around ₩800 per dollar. In recent years, the rate has usually run a little under ₩800. A current exchange rate at an English bank fluctuates around ₩1,200 per pound.

Dialogue 2 ◯◯ *On another occasion James Park runs out of money and wants to withdraw some cash from his savings account. He gets some assistance from the teller in charge*

행원: 어떻게 오셨어요?
박: 현금을 찾으러 왔는데요.
행원: 예금을 찾으려면, 도장과 통장이 필요해요.
박: 예, 통장은 있는데, 도장이 없는데요.
행원: 그럼, 이 예금 청구서에다가 액수를 기입하세요.
　　　 그리고, 서명을 하세요.
박: 잘 알았습니다. 이제 다 됐습니다.
　　　 가능하면, 만원 짜리 지폐로 다섯 장 주세요.
행원: 그럼, 저기 소파에 앉아서 잠깐만 기다려 주세요.
　　　　　　(한참후에)
행원: James Park 손님, 여기 통장과 돈을 가지고 가세요.
박: 예, 감사합니다. 아가씨, 수고하세요.
행원: 안녕히 가세요.

Vocabulary

어떻게	how	서명하다	sign one's name
현금	cash		
현금을 찾다	withdraw money	가능하면	if possible
필요하다	need (something)	만원 짜리	worth 10,000 won
없다	don't have		
청구서	withdrawal slip	지폐	paper bill
액수	amount	행원	bank teller
그리고	and	돈	money
		아가씨	Miss

Language points

Another purpose ending -(으)러

This phrasal ending is used with action verbs and indicates the purpose of an action. It is usually accompanied by such verbs as 가다, 오다, or other composite verbs combined with these two. This ending also signifies "in order to" in English.

저금을 하러 여기에 왔다.	I came here to make a deposit.
학생들은 점심 먹으러 식당에 갔어요.	Students went to the restaurant for lunch.
학생들이 공부하러 도서관에 갔어요.	Students went to the library to study.

The intentional/conditional ending -(으)려면

This ending combines -으려고 and -면, and translates as "If one is going to do something (i.e., if one intends to do something), then . . ." It is usually used with action verbs.

돈을 찾으려면 은행에 가야해요.
If you want to withdraw money, you have to go to the bank.

연필을 사려면 문방구점에 가야해요.
If you want to buy pencils, you have to go a stationery store.

예금을 하려면 비밀번호를 적어야해요.
If you want to make a deposit, you have to write the PIN number.

The postposition -에다가

This postposition, when attached to nouns, indicates a specific surface on (or onto) which something is written. The English equivalent of it is "in," "on," or "onto." The final word -가 can sometimes be deleted.

공책에다(가) 쓰세요.	Please write in the notebook.
예금청구서에다가 액수를 쓰세요.	Please write the amount on the withdrawal slip.

The noun suffix - 짜리

This noun suffix, when attached to monetary units, indicates "a thing worth . . ."

백원 짜리 두장	two ₩100 bills
만원 짜리 세장	three ₩10,000 bills
이십불 짜리 열장	ten $20 bills

The sentence ending - 이 필요하다

This ending literally means "something is needed." Although in a Korean sentence this verb takes two kinds of subject (a person and a thing), the second subject becomes the object in its English translation.

나는 연필이 필요한데요.	I need a pencil.
통장을 개설하려면,	You need a wooden stamp if you
도장이 필요해요.	wish to open an account.

Exercises

12 Someone asks you where the members of staff in your office went during their lunch hour. Tell him that each individual went to the following places to do the following things. Use the conjunction -(으)러 in your answer.

a Mr. Kim went to the bank to withdraw some cash.
b Section Chief Lee went to the staffroom for a break.
c Secretary Hong went to the payroll office to pick up her pay check.

13 A friend of yours lost her purse somewhere in the supermarket. Advise her to go to the cashier's desk.

14 A friend of yours doesn't know what to do in order to withdraw cash with his check book. Advise him to write in the PIN number and sign his name on the form. In your answer, use the postposition -에다가.

15 You are in a bank and want to withdraw ₩65,000 in cash. Tell the teller you'd like five 10,000 won units and three 5,000 won units.

16 You meet a foreigner at a local bank and you notice that she is at a loss as to what she needs in order to open a savings account. Advise her that she needs the following things:

a a wooden stamp
b passport
c PIN number

17 Rearrange the words to make sense.

a 찾으려면, 예금을, 필요해요, 도장이
b 이름칸에, 찍으세요, 비밀번호도, 쓰시고, 도장을
c 짜리, 만원, 필요해요, 다섯장

18 Translate the following dialogue into Korean:

A: How can I help you?
B: I came here to make a deposit.
A: Just fill out the form over there.
B: All right.

19 Complete the dialogue:

A: 어떻게 오셨어요?
B:
A: 얼마 찾으시겠어요?
B:
A: 그럼, 저기 청구서에다가 액수를 쓰세요.
B:
A: 잠깐만 기다리세요.
B:

20 Reading passage　⬛⬛　One Saturday morning, James Park goes to the bank near the hotel where he is staying. He wants to withdraw some cash, but is told that he needs to show some sort of proof of his identity. So, he goes back to his hotel room, then hurries back to the bank. But when he arrives at the bank, it is closed. Try to figure our what problem he ran into and what he had to do.

어느 토요일 오전이었다. 제일금융회사에서 일하는 James Park 씨는 현금을 찾으러 근처에 있는 은행에 갔다. 예금을 찾으려면, 여권이 필요했다. 그러나, 여권을 호텔방에 놓아두고 와서, 현금을 찾을 수가 없었다. 그래서, 다시 호텔방에 가서 여권을 가지고 은행에 급히 갔지만, 은행은 문을 닫았다. 기분이 별로 좋지 않았다.

Key words

제일금융회사	First Banking Company	급히	hurriedly
현금	cash	은행	bank
필요하다	need	문을 닫다	close the door
놓아 두다	leave behind	현금을 찾다	withdraw money

13 다방에서 친구 만나기
Meeting friends at a Dabang

By the end of this lesson you should be able to:
- make an apology
- talk about daily routines with friends
- use the conjunctions -기 전에, -기 때문에
- use the double past tense -었(았)었
- use the modification marker -ㄹ(을)
- use the sentence endings -아(어/여)야 되다, -군요
- use the particle -전에
- use the stative verb 많다
- use the postposition -한테

Dialogue 1 🔲🔲 *At a Dabang (Korean tearoom) Jane Adams runs into Dal Hoon Lee, a university student she has recently met. He is late for a meeting because of heavy traffic*

달훈: 늦어서 미안해요.
제인: 천만에요.
달훈: 오래 전에 왔어요?
제인: 아니요, 나도 조금 전에 왔어요.
달훈: 버스로 오는데, 교통이 막혀서 빨리 올 수 없었어요.
제인: 서울 거리는 너무 차가 많아서 복잡해요.
달훈: 고려대학교 정문 앞은 완전히 막혔어요.
제인: 그래요? 또 학생들이 데모했어요?
달훈: 아니오. 교통사고가 정문 앞에서 났었어요.
제인: 저는 교통이 밀리기 전에 왔어요.

Vocabulary

늦다	late	고려대학교	Korea university
미안하다	feel sorry for	완전히	completely
오래전에	a while ago	데모하다	protest
조금전에	a little while ago	교통사고	traffic accident
버스	bus	정문	main gate
교통	traffic	사고가 나다	an accident occurred
막히다	jammed		
빨리	quickly	밀리다	backed up in a line
서울거리	Seoul streets		
복잡하다	crowded	앞	front
차	car	전에	ago

Language points

The temporal conjunction -기 전에

This conjunction, when attached to the action verb stem, indicates "a time before the present." It is equivalent to the English expression "before one does something," or "before doing something," as in the sentence "He returned home before it rained."

비가 오기 전에 집에 갑시다.	Let's go home before it starts to rain.
늦기 전에 회의에 갑시다.	Let's go to the meeting before we're late.
연말이 되기 전에 고향에 가겠어요.	I'll go to my hometown before the year's through.

The particle 전에

This is used with the word for the various time units ("minutes," "hours," etc.) and indicates "at a time before the present." It is equivalent to "ago."

기차가 오분 전에 도착했어요.	The train arrived five minutes ago.
한시간 전에는 날씨가 아주 좋았어요.	The weather was very good even an hour ago.

The double past tense marker -었(았)었

The past tense marker -었 can be used twice when some event is completed prior to another event in the past. It can also be used when the completion of an event has no effect on the sentence uttered.

그분은 3년 전에 결혼했었어요.	He had married (someone) three years ago.
두 시간 전에 김선생님 여기에 왔었어요.	Mr. Kim had come here two hours ago.
한국에 있을 때, 한국 음식을 많이 먹었었다.	While in Korea, I used to have Korean food a lot.

Another causal conjunction -기 때문에

This conjunction connects two sentences forming a cause and effect relationship. It is interchangeable with the conjunctions -아/어/여서 and -(으)니까, explained in Lessons 3 and 12.

요즈음 학기말이기 때문에 지금 바빠요.
Since these are the last days of the semester, I am extremely busy.

김사장님은 회의가 있기 때문에 지금 바빠요.
Since President Kim has a meeting, he is busy right now.

차가 고장이 났기 때문에 늦게 왔어요.
Since the car was broken down, I came late.

But this form cannot be used with a request sentence.

(X) 비가 많이 오기 때문에 밖에 나가지 마세요.	Since it's raining heavily, don't go outside.

The stative verb 많다

This verb refers to a great quantity of things or persons. It is equivalent to "much" and "many." But the verb is subject to various changes in form in a sentence. The adverb 많이 and the adjective 많은 are derived from this verb.

교실에 학생들이 많아요. (verb)   ⎫   There are many
많은 학생들이 교실에 있어요. (adjective) ⎬   students in the
교실에 학생들이 많이 있어요. (adverb)   ⎭   classroom.

Exercises

1 You are late for an appointment with your friend at a Korean tearoom (Dabang). Apologize to him.

2 Your boss asks you why you were late for a business meeting this morning. Tell him that because the traffic was terrible, you couldn't make it on time.

3 Someone is looking for the foreman (Mr. Kim), and you think that you saw him in his office only a few minutes ago. Tell him that he was in his office just a short time ago.

4 You and some colleagues go for a picnic. In the middle of the picnic the sky suddenly turns cloudy and threatens to rain. Tell the others to go inside the building before it starts raining.

5 Correct your friend's grammar:

a 지금 비는 와서 안으로 들어 갑시다.
b 바람가 많이 불기 때문에 건물 안에 들어 가세요.
c 학생들이 교실에 많이다.
d 이사장님은 많는 돈이 있다.

6 Rerrange the words of the dialogue to make sense:

a 밀려서, 교통이, 서울역, 앞은, 혼잡하다, 언제나
b 학생들이, 데모해서, 시내에서, 복잡하다, 교통이
c 서울에서, 먹었었다, 많은, 한국음식을

7 Translate the following dialogue into Korean:

A: I'm sorry to be late.
B: That's all right.
A: I took the bus, but it couldn't go fast because the traffic was congested.
B: That's too bad. Were university students rioting?
A: Oh, no. There was a traffic accident in front of City Hall.

8 Complete the dialogue:

A: 어제 어디 갔었어요?
B:

A: 교통은 밀리지 않았었어요?

·B:

　보통 때보다 두 시간 더 걸렸었어요.

A: 교통사고가 . 났었어요?

B: 　학생들이 데모를 했었어요.

Culture point

Koreans are generally flexible about keeping appointments. It is not uncommon to show up well over 30 minutes late for an appointment, whether business or personal. One of the major reasons for their flexibility seems to be deeply rooted in their past lifestyle. Not long ago, only a very small percentage of Koreans owned a car. The majority of Koreans had to rely on public transport whose hourly operations were extremely unpredictable. Thus, for many years, they had to live with the reality of never really knowing when they would arrive. Although nowadays over 60 percent of Seoulites own a vehicle of one type or another, their past experience is well ingrained in their modern lifestyle. Even if one has a car, appalling traffic conditions on Seoul streets cause a whole set of new problems. To minimize this sense of uncertainty, a foreigner is advised to use the subway, one of the easiest means of public transport, which runs at pre-scheduled times. Korean subways are also clean and quiet, and make stops at every major point in Seoul.

Dialogue 2 ▱ *Jane begins to understand why Dal Hoon has been so busy lately when he mentions that he is tutoring his younger brother in English every week*

여종업원:	안녕하세요? 뭘 드시겠어요?
제인:	저는 인삼차 한 잔 하겠어요.
달훈:	저는 콜라 한 잔 하겠어요.
여종업원:	예, 곧 갖다 드리겠습니다.
달훈:	요즈음 어떻게 지내세요?
제인:	그저 그렇게 지내요. 달훈씨는 어때요?
달훈:	요새 방학이지만, 할 일이 많아요.
제인:	무슨 일이 그렇게 많아요?
달훈:	내 동생한테 영어 개인지도를 해야해요.
제인:	일주일에 몇 시간씩 가르쳐요?
달훈:	4시간씩 가르쳐요.
제인:	아, 그래요. 힘들겠군요.

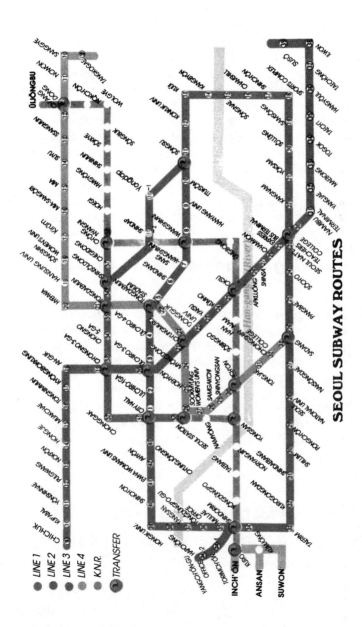

SEOUL SUBWAY ROUTES

Vocabulary

들다	have (food)	그렇게	like that
인삼차	ginseng tea	한테	to someone (younger person)
요즈음	these days		
그저 그렇게	so-so	영어	English
요새	lately	개인지도	tutoring
방학	vacation	일 주일	one week
할 일	things to do	가르치다	teach
무슨 일	what kind of work	4시간씩	every four hours
		힘들다	difficult

Language points

Two forms of the verb "to bring something for someone" in Korean

These are 갖다주다 and 갖다 드리다. 갖다주다 is used when a speaker requests something for himself or when when he gives something to someone who is younger or lower in social status. However, 갖다 드리다 is used when a speaker does so for someone whose social status is higher or to anyone present to whom he wants to look polite.

물 좀 갖다 주세요	Please bring me some water.
네, 곧 갖다 드리지요.	Yes, I'll bring it right away.
이 책 저분한테 갖다 드리세요.	Please take this book to him over there.

The modification marker - ㄹ(을)

This marker is used when a noun follows action and adjectival verbs, and indicates the future tense.

마실 물이 없어요.	There is no water to drink.
읽을 책이 많아요.	There are many books to read.
이번 주말에 할 일이 많아요.	I have a lot of work to do this weekend.

The postposition -한테

This postposition is used to indicate the receiver of a certain action of a verb. It accompanies a person. Note that the postposition -에게 is interchangeable with -한테

누구한테(에게) 편지 썼어요?	Who did you write a letter to?
형님한테(에게) 편지 썼어요?	I wrote the letter to my older brother.

The obligation ending -아(어/여)야 되다

This ending is used to express an obligation or necessity in respect of a certain event, when attached to the verb stem of the sentence. It is interchangeable with the ending -어(아/여)야 되다

지금 이 음식을 먹어야 돼요.	Now I have to eat this food.
내일은 날씨가 좋아야 돼요.	Tomorrow's weather should be good.
매일 개인 지도를 해야 돼요.	I have to do private tutoring every day.

The noun particle -씩

This particle is attached directly to a number or to any number made with the noun counter. It means "each," "respectively," "apiece."

하루에 두 시간씩 한국어 공부해요.	I study the Korean language for two hours every day.
학생들은 셋씩 도서관에 와요.	Students come to the library in groups of three.

The exclamatory ending -군요

This ending is used with any verb and indicates a speaker's delight, wonder, astonishment, or surprise. It is interchangeable with -ㄴ(는/은)데요 explained in Lesson 6. The suffix 는 can be inserted when an action verb precedes.

오늘은 눈이 많이 오는군요!	It's snowing a lot today!
어제 일요일인데, 학교 갔었군요!	Yesterday was Sunday, but you went to school!

이 일은 아주 힘들겠군요!	This work must be very difficult to do!
이 물건값은 아주 싸군요!	This merchandise is very cheap (inexpensive)!

Exercises

9 You are at a Dabang and the waiter is ready to take your order. Ask him to bring you a cup of coffee.

10 You borrowed a book from a friend which he checked out of the city library. You tell him that you will return it there when you've read it.

11 A friend asks you how you're doing these days. Respond to his question.

12 A friend asks whether you are free today. Tell him that you have a lot to read for a meeting.

13 You bought office supplies at a stationery store and one of your office colleagues wants to borrow some of them. Tell him that you gave them to the following people:

a pencil to a younger brother
b ruler to an uncle
c notebook to an older sister

14 You are tutoring two high school students (Young Hee and Jae Min) in English conversation. A friend asks how many hours you tutor each student every week. Respond to his question, according to the information below!

a Young Hee for three hours
b Jae Min for two hours

15 Someone is telling you that he works 12 hours a week. Express your surprise, saying that the job must be extremely tiring.

16 A friend of yours persuades you to go out to a park this Saturday afternoon. Tell her that you have the following things to do:

a take a rest
b read a book
c go to a movie with your brother

17 Translate the following dialogue into colloquial English:

A: How've you been doing these days?
B: I've been busy.
A: What kind of work makes you that busy?
B: I've got lots of meetings these days.
A: Oh, really? It must be very tiring.

18 Complete the dialogue below:

A: 요즈음 바쁜 일 있어요?
B:
A: 무슨 일이 그렇게 많아요?
B:
A: 일주일에 몇 시간씩 가르치세요?
B:
A: 그럼, 힘들겠군요.

19 Reading passage ▭▭ Jane meets a friend of hers at a Dabang (Korean tearoom). She is very late. After talking together about something to do over the weekend, she goes home. Because of the traffic problem, she changes her mind and goes home by taxi instead of by bus. Try to figure out what kind of weekend plan they discussed and why Jane took a taxi home.

제인(Jane)은 어느 금요일 저녁에 친구와 다방에서 만났다. 친구가 30분 늦게 와서 많이 기다려야 했다. 친구는 커피를 마시고, 제인은 인삼차를 한 잔 마셨다. 둘은 주말여행에 관하여 이야기했다. 집으로 돌아오는 길에 버스를 탔는데, 교통이 막혀서 버스가 움직일 수 없었다. 그래서, 도중에 버스에서 내려서 택시를 타고 집으로 돌아왔다.

Key Words

늦게 오다	arrive late	막히다	be jammed
주말여행	weekend trip	움직이다	move around
관하여	about	도중에	on the way
길	way		

14 호텔에서
At the hotel

By the end of this lesson you should be able to:
- check in at a hotel
- use the long negation form -지 못하다
- use the sentence endings -밖에 없다, -아(어/여)보다,
  ㄹ(을)지 모르겠다, -고 싶다
- use the postposition -(으)로

Dialogue 1 🔲🔲 *Mr. Anderson and his friend, Mr. Taylor, try
to check in at a hotel for a couple of nights. They prefer to take
rooms with single beds at an affordable price*

접수계: 어서 오세요. 몇 분이십니까?
앤더슨: 두 사람인데, 방 있어요?
접수계: 오시기 전에 예약하셨어요?
앤더슨: 아니요. 예약하지 못했어요.
접수계: 그래요. 잠깐만 기다리세요.
　　　　아, 빈 방이 몇 개 있습니다.
　　　　그런데, 침대방은 없고 온돌방밖에 없는데요.
테일러: 앤더슨, 온돌방이 괜찮겠어요?
앤더슨: 나는 온돌방에서 못 자는데요.
테일러: 그럼, 다른 호텔로 가 보겠습니다.
접수계: 예, 다음에 또 들르세요.

Vocabulary

몇 분	how many persons (honorific)	온돌방	room with built-in stone heat
방	room	괜찮다	OK
예약하다	make a reservation	다른	different

빈 방	empty room	호텔	hotel
몇 개	several	-못 하다	cannot do
들르다	drop by	-밖에 없다	nothing but
침대방	room with Western-style beds		

Language points

The long negation form -지 못하다

Two ways of negating Korean verbs have been introduced. These were -안 (short form) seen in Lesson 1 and -지 않다 (long form) seen in Lesson 10. In this lesson another negative marker 못 is introduced. This negative ending, mostly used with action verbs, indicates "one's failing or inability to do something," as in the sentence "John failed to pass the test because he didn't study hard." There are two forms of negation:

Verb		Short form	Long form	
가다	go	못 가다	가지 못하다	unable to go
먹다	eat	못 먹다	먹지 못하다	unable to eat
읽다	read	못 읽다	읽지 못하다	unable to read

The negative sentence ending -밖에 없다

This ending, followed by a noun, means "nothing but," "only."

교실에 여학생밖에 없습니다.	There are only girls in the classroom.
온돌방밖에 없는데요.	We have nothing but the Ondol rooms.

The compound form -아(어/여) 보다

This form is used to express a trial or experiment by the action verbs of a sentence, as in "Do you want to try on this sweater?" The tense is reflected in the second verb 보다, meaning "to see how it is."

저 청바지를 입어 보세요. (present)
Try on the jeans over there.

이번 일요일에 창경원에 가 보겠어요. (future)
I'll try going to the zoo this Sunday.

미국 식당에서 일해 보셨어요? (past)
Have you ever worked for an American-style restaurant?

The postposition -(으)로

This postposition denotes a destination to which one moves or to which something moves. The equivalent in English is "toward." It is interchangeable with the postposition -에 explained in Lesson 1. 으 is inserted for nouns ending in a consonant (except ㄹ).

정문 앞에 있는 분식집으로   Let's go to the snack house by
  갑시다.   the main gate.
이 버스는 어디로 갑니까? Where does the bus go?
그 사람은 어디로 갔어요? Where did the man go?

Exercises

1 A clerk at the hotel counter asks whether you made a room reservation. Respond to his question, saying that you failed to do so. Use the long negation form in your answer.

2 A friend wants you to return the book you borrowed. Tell him that you haven't finished reading it. This time, use the short negation form.

3 You have been busy all morning and a colleague asks you whether you have had a coffee break. Tell her that you haven't taken it.

4 Someone asks you whether you saw the movie *ET*. Tell him that you couldn't watch it because you were too busy.

5 A friend of yours wants to borrow ₩50,000 from you. Tell him that you only have ₩30,000 in your pocket.

6 You want to try on a nice-looking sweater at the store. Ask the salesman whether you can do so.

7 Someone asks you whether you went to Dream Land in Seoul. Tell him that you have not been there yet.

8 The hotel clerk asks you whether you can take the Ondol room (floor-heated room). Tell him that you can't sleep on the Ondol floor.

9 A hotel clerk says that all the rooms are booked for the night. Suggest that you and your friend go to another place across the street.

10 Reorder the words of the dialogue to make sense:

A: 두개, 침대방, 있어요?
B: 여기는, 없으니까, 침대방이, 여관으로, 다른, 가 보세요
A: 그럼, 있어요?, 온돌방은
B: 세개, 온돌방은, 있습니다, 예

11 Translate the following dialogue into Korean:

A: How many are you?
B: We're three.
A: Would you (mind) check(ing) into the Ondol room?
B: No. Since we're foreigners, we'll check into rooms with beds.
A: We don't have any rooms with beds.
B: Really? We'll go to the other hotel nearby.

Culture point

There are lots of modern hotels in downtown Seoul. If you buy a tourist map of Seoul city at a newsstand, you can easily locate these hotels on the map because they are marked in both Korean and English. The major ones providing good quality, Western-style service are the Sinra Hotel, Chosun Hotel, Hotel Lotte, and Seoul Hilton Hotel, to mention only a few. These hotels are equipped with modern facilities such as all-year-round heating and air-conditioning, in-house restaurants and bars, laundry, beauty and barber shops, and agencies offering domestic travel services and foreign exchange services.

You can choose between various classes of hotel, depending on your travel budget. Deluxe hotels such as the Chosun or the Seoul Hilton have rooms ranging from $400 (double) up to $500 a night, while first-class hotels such as Sinra and Lotte charge an average of $300 a night for a double. Of course, second- and third-class hotels charge much less, at $100 a night. All rooms have private bathrooms, two single beds or one double bed, phones, radio and TV sets, and closets.

You don't have to be afraid, even if your Korean isn't good enough, to have a brief conversation with a Korean waiter or waitress. Most hotel personnel (if not all) are able to speak some English, and they are also trained to help foreign travelers.

It is always a good idea to study the pamphlets for foreign tourists in Korea before you get there. These pamphlets are usually available at any of the Korean Consulate offices, located in the major cities of the U.S.A. Your knowledge of hotels and of other tourist needs and interests will help make your choice easier and your stay more enjoyable.

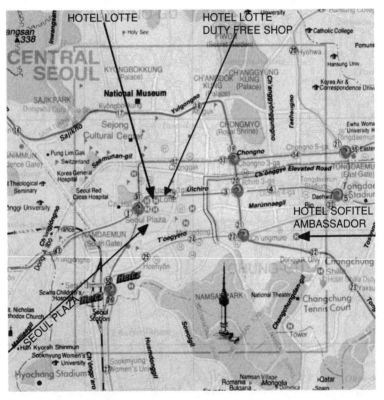

Dialogue 2 🔲🔲 *Mr. Anderson and Mr. Taylor go to an inn across the street and succeed in checking into a big room with two single beds*

앤더슨: 이 여관에 빈 방 있어요?
접수계: 방이 있을지 모르겠군요. 잠깐만 기다리세요.
　　　　예, 온돌방과 침대방 다 있습니다.

앤더슨: 저희들은 침대방을 쓰고 싶은데요.
접수계: 침대방은 크니까, 3만원 내셔야 됩니다.
테일러: 예, 알겠습니다. 침대방 하나만 주세요.
접수계: 여기 성함하고 주소, 그리고 여권 번호 적어 주세요.
테일러/앤더슨: 예, 그러지요.
테일러: 우리 방은 몇 호실입니까?
접수계: 406호실입니다. 열쇠 여기 있습니다.
접수계: 아가씨, 감사합니다.

Vocabulary

여관	inn	하나만	only one
모르겠다	do not know	여권 번호	passport number
다 있다	have all	몇 호실	what room number
저희들	we (humble)	406호실	room #406
(하고)싶다	want/wish	열쇠	key

Language points

The sentence ending -ㄹ(을)지 모르겠다

This ending changes the final verb and is used to incorporate an interrogative or "if" -sentence into a main sentence. The English translation is "One knows/doesn't know whether/if+sentence." With all action verbs, it expresses the future tense.

언제 회의가 있을지 모르겠어요.	I don't know when the meeting is held.
그 분이 집에 있을지 몰라요.	I don't know whether he will be staying home.
그 일이 어떻게 될지 모르겠어요.	I don't know how that work will turn out.

The sentence ending -고 싶다

This ending expresses a speaker's wish to do something. It is equivalent to the English infinitive phrase "want to do," or "would like to do."

무슨 음식을 들고 싶으세요?	What kind of food would you like to have?
새 구두를 사고 싶어요.	I want to buy new shoes.
지금 무엇을 .하고 싶으세요?	What would you like to do right now?

The noun particle -호실

This particle, when attached to a Sino-Korean number, indicates a room number.

3호실이 어딥니까?	Where is room #3?
102호실은 어느 쪽입니까?	Which is the way to (Which direction is) room #102?

Exercises

12 A colleague asks you if you know when a staff meeting will be. Using -지몰라요, tell her that you do not know.

13 Next month you expect to get a huge bonus in your pay check. A friend of yours wonders how you will spend it. Tell her that you want to spend it by doing the following things:

a buying a new suit
b buying a birthday gift for your girlfriend
c buying three books

14 Before arriving at the hotel, you made a room reservation. Ask the clerk what number your room is.

15 One of your friends checked in prior to your arrival at the hotel. At the hotel counter you wonder which room he checked into. Ask the clerk his room number.

16 A group of foreigners are at the hotel counter, and you are there as an interpreter for them. Ask the clerk whether there are rooms with beds available for five people.

17 Tell the clerk that you need two rooms with beds and one Ondol (floor-heated) room.

18 Translate this dialogue into Korean:

A: Do you have any rooms with beds in this hotel?
B: No, we've only Ondol rooms here.
A: How much do you charge for one Ondol room?
B: It's ₩30,000.

19 Complete the following dialogue:

A: 이 여관에 침대방 있어요?
B:
A: 두개만 주세요.
B:
A: 한 방에 3만원짜리는 없어요?
B:
A: 그럼, 한 방에 4만원짜리 주세요.
B:

20 Reading passage ▣▣ Mr. Anderson was about to check in at the hotel reception. But he could not check in because he forgot to bring something that he was supposed to have with him. So, he made a phone call to a friend who knew where it was. With his friend's help, he cleared up the problem. Try to figure out what he forgot to bring with him and how his friend helped him.

앤더슨씨는 대전에 혼자 출장 갔다. 대전에 도착하여 호텔에 투숙하려고 했으나, 여권을 가지고 가지 않아서 투숙을 할 수 없었다. 그래서, 서울 사무실에 있는 동료 직원 헨리(Henry)에게 전화를 했다. 헨리가 앤더슨씨의 책상 서랍에서 여권을 찾아 번호를 알려 주어서, 그 번호를 숙박명부에 적을 수 있었다. 그가 투숙한 침대방은 크고 깨끗해서 값이 비쌌다. 그렇지만, 방이 조용해서 잠을 잘 잘 수가 있었다.

Key words

출장가다	go on a business trip	번호	number
투숙하다	check in (at a hotel)	숙박부	information sheet
여권	passport	침대방	room with (Western-style) beds
서랍	drawer		

15 한국의 날씨
Korea's weather

By the end of this lesson you should be able to:
- talk about characteristics of Korea's four seasons
- use the nominalizing suffix -기
- use the sentence endings -는 때가 있다, -네요 -ㄴ(은/는) 것같다
- use the compound verbs -러 가다/오다, 아(어/여)지다

Dialogue 1   Roy Kim has recently arrived in Seoul and is talking with his tour guide, Jenny Lee

로야: 한국의 기후는 어때요?
제니: 대체로 따뜻하고, 사계절이 분명해요.
로야: 봄은 언제부터 시작되어요?
제니: 봄은 3월부터 시작되지요. 봄이 되면 꽃이 피기 시작해요.
로야: 3월에는 눈이 오는 때가 없어요?
제니: 그럼요. 3월이면 벌써 따뜻해져요.
로야: 미국에는 4월에도 눈이 오는 때가 있어요.
제니: 그래요? 굉장히 춥겠네요.
로야: 예, 춥지요. 그래서, 사람들은 여름이 빨리 오기를 기다려요.

Vocabulary

기후	weather	월(달)	month
따뜻하다	warm	눈	snow
사계절	four seasons	눈이 오다	it snows
분명하다	distinctive	벌써	already
봄	spring	미국	America
언제부터	since when	굉장히	extremely

시작하다	begin	춥다	cold
꽃	flowers	여름	summer
피다	bloom	한국	Korea

Language points

The nominalizing suffix -기

This suffix is attached to the stem of action verbs and expresses the gerund ("-ing") or "to"-infinitive in English.

시작하다	begin	시작하기	beginning
공부하다	study	공부하기	studying

The nominal marker converts a verb into a noun equivalent, so that the nominalized expression -기 functions grammatically like a noun. Thus, it can be taken as either the subject or object of certain types of verb. Here are a few examples where -기 is used as the object of a verb:

시작하다	begin to do something *or* begin doing something
비가 오기(를) 시작했다.	It began to rain.
그는 아침을 먹기 시작했다.	He began to have breakfast.
기다리다.	wait for someone/something to do
사람들은 비가 멈추기를 기다려요.	People wait for the rain to stop.
학생들은 수업이 끝나기를 기다렸어요.	Students wait for class to finish.

The sentence ending -는 때가 있다

The suffix 는, when attached to the stem of action verbs, modifies the noun 때 ("time") and means "there is a time when someone does something."

Jane은 학교에 지각하는 때가 많다.	Jane is often late for school.
4월에도 눈이 오는 때가 있어요.	It sometimes snows in April.

Another exclamatory ending -네요

Two exclamatory endings have been introduced so far: -은/는데요 in Lesson 10 and -(는)군요 in Lesson 13. Here is another ending of a similar kind which indicates a speaker's delight, wonder, surprise, etc.

학생들이 많이 지각했네요!	Many students are late!
106번 버스가 저기에 오네요!	Bus #106 is coming over there!
내일은 날씨가 좋겠네요.!	Tomorrow's weather will be good!

Exercises

1 You are standing in the hallway, and someone you know asks what you are up to. Tell him that you are waiting for the following people to come out of a meeting in progress:

a Jane Kim
b Thomas Moon
c Teacher Lee

2 You have been very busy and haven't seen one of your friends for weeks. He asks what kept you so busy. Tell him that you have started the following:

a reading a Korean novel
b studying the Korean language
c dating a girlfriend

3 A Korean student asks you what the weather is like in April in your hometown. Tell him that, even in April, it sometimes snows.

4 You are delighted because the bus you were waiting for just came to a halt at the station. Say that bus #123 just came in.

5 You are at a meeting and you realize many of your colleagues are absent. Show your surprise.

6 Correct your friend's grammar:

a 그는 여름이 오기가 기다린다.
b 갑자기 비가 오기은 시작했다.
c Jane은 때로는 술을 많이 마시은 때가 있다.

7 Rearrange the words of the dialogue so they make sense:

A: 눈이, 지역도, 여름에, 오는, 있다
B: 오기를, 가을이, 사람들이, 기다려요
C: 한국의, 사계절은, 기후가, 분명하다

8 Translate the following dialogue into Korean:

A: What are Korean summers like?
B: It's usually hot.
A: Does it rain a lot?
B: Yes, it rains a lot because there's a monsoon in the summer.

9 Complete the following dialogue:

A: 한국의 가을 날씨는 어때요?
B:
A: 사람들은 가을에 무얼 해요?
B:
A: 수영하러 가는 사람도 있어요?
B:

Culture point

Korea's weather belongs to the temperate zone and its four seasons are quite distinct. The warm spring weather is heralded by gold-banded lilies blooming from mid-March in the southern region to early April in the central region, which includes Seoul. A sudden cold wave in spring may, however, take many people by surprise. Summer begins in June when the Korean peninsula is under the influence of the monsoon. The Korean summer is notorious for its long rainy spell, which usually takes up the whole of July: "hot and humid" is characteristic of Korea's summer weather. It is during this season that typhoons may at times threaten to inflict heavy damage on the Korean peninsula. After the dreary days of summer, autumn arrives. Its weather is very mild and the sky high and clear. Travelers must not miss the ripening Korean apples and pears in the orchards in autumn. Winter usually begins in mid-November in the northern region. At times heavy snow may accumulate but for the most part winter is dry and cold.

Dialogue 2 🔲🔲 *Roy asks Jenny about Korea's autumn weather*

로이: 한국의 가을 날씨는 어때요?
제니: 가을 날씨는 맑고 시원해요.

로이: 가을에 사람들은 어디로 놀러가요?
제니: 어떤 사람들은 산에 가고, 어떤 사람들은 낚시질 가요.
로이: 산에는 무얼 하러 가요?
제니: 단풍 구경하러 가요.
로이: 그럼, 언제부터 추워지기 시작해요?
제니: 우리 지역은 12월 초순부터 추워지기 시작해요.
로이: 아, 밖이 어두워지고, 비가 오는 것 같아요.
제니: 맞아요. 안으로 들어 가야겠어요.

Vocabulary

가을	autumn	12월	December
날씨	weather	초순	first one-third of a month
맑다	clear		
시원하다	cool	밖	outside
놀러가다	go to hang out	어두워지다	get dark
어떤	some/certain	비가 오다	it rains
산	mountain	맞다	correct
낚시질	fishing	안으로	(toward) inside
단풍	foliage	들어가다	go inside
구경하다	watch	사람	people
지역	region		

Language points

The compound verb -러 가다/오다

This ending combines some action verbs with the verbs 가다/오다 and means "go/come to do something."

학생들이 도서관에 공부하러 가요.	Students go to the library to study.
친구들이 우리 집에 놀러 왔어요.	Friends came to my house to do nothing.
운동장에 배구하러 갔어요.	They went to the field to play volleyball.

The question word 어떤

This word modifies the noun which follows it. Its translation depends upon the context. For example, in a declarative sentence the word means "certain or some," but in a question it means "what kind of . . ."

어떤 학생들은 도서관에서 공부하고 있어요.	Some students are studying at the library.
어떤 학생이 복도에 있어요.	A certain student is standing in the hall.
어떤 학생이 복도에 있어요?	Which student is standing in the hall?

The personal pronoun 우리

Koreans tend to use 우리 ("we") to indicate their family relationships with someone, instead of using 저/나 ("I"). They believe that a sense of collectivity or sharing about one's family is extended not only to the home itself, but also to other social institutions (e.g., school, company, restaurant, etc). Therefore, the Korean personal pronoun 우리 translates into English as "we" or "I."

우리 집에 내일 저녁에 놀러 오세요.	Please come and visit my home tomorrow evening.
우리는 내일 아주 바빠요.	We are very busy tomorrow.
우리 회사 직원들이 일요일에 소풍가요.	The staff of our company go on a picnic (on) Sunday.

The compound verb ending -아(어/여) 지다

This verb ending is attached to the stem of the verb and adds a dependent meaning to the given verb. It indicates a process of change or "becoming" from one condition to another.

많다 many 많아지다 become more → 사람들이 많아졌어요. The number of people increased (*lit.* became larger)

길다 long 길어지다 become   → 여름이 되면 날이 길어져요.
             longer   When summer comes, the
                                    days get longer (*lit.* when
                                    it becomes a summer, the
                                    daylights became longer)

예쁘다 pretty 예뻐지다 become → 요즈음 그 여학생 얼굴이
             prettier   예뻐졌어요.
                                    She's became more pretty
                                    recently (*lit.* these days
                                    she became prettier)

The sentence ending - ㄴ(은/는) 것 같다

This ending is attached to the stem of the verb and means "It
seems/appears to be ..." When the suffix -ㄴ(은) is attached to
descriptive verbs and the linking verb (이다/아니다), it expresses
the present tense. But when the same suffix is attached to action
verbs, it expresses the past tense. Finally, the suffix -는 is used with
action verbs to create the present tense.

이것은 비싼 것 같다.   This seems (to be) expensive.

오늘은 날씨가 좋은 것 같다.   Today's weather seems (to
                                    be) good.

저 사람은 한국사람인 것 같다. That person appears to be a
                                    Korean.

저 사람은 한국사람이 아닌   That person does not appear
   것 같다.   to be a Korean.

그 학생이 책을 읽은 것   The student seems to have
   같아요.   read the book.

John이 미국에 돌아간   John seems to have returned
   것 같아요.   to America.

밖에 지금 비가 오는 것 같아요. It seems to be raining outside
                                      now.

Exercises

10 On your way to Chongro, you run across a friend of yours on
a Seoul street. Respond to his question, "What are you doing in
Chongro?" Tell him that you are going to do the following things
there:

a buy books
b meet friends
c spend time with friends

11 You have lost contact with Harry lately, and someone asks you his whereabouts. Tell him that he seems to have done the following:

a returned to America
b broken up with his girlfriend
c gone on a business trip
d fallen ill

12 Someone asks you whether there are students studying at such a late hour in the library. Tell him that particular students from America are studying there.

13 You did not have a chance to meet one of your colleagues lately. When you unexpectedly meet him, you notice that he looks younger than before. Compliment him.

14 Say that, now summer has begun, the days are getting longer.

15 Translate the following dialogue into Korean:

A: What are Korean autumns like?
B: It's usually clear.
A: Does it often snow in autumn?
B: No, it starts to snow in December.
A: What do people do in autumn?
B: They go mountain climbing.

16 Complete the following dialogue:

A:
B: 한국의 가을 날씨는 보통 이래요.
A:
B: 단풍구경하러 설악산에 가겠어요.
A:
B: 아니오. 친구들과 같이 갈거예요.

17 *Reading passage* ☐☐ The following text discusses Korea's four seasons. It suggests things to do in each. Try to figure out the advantages and disadvantages of each season.

한국의 기후는 대체로 사계절이 분명해요. 봄에는 산과 들에
꽃이 만발해서 아름다워요. 사람들은 봄에 산으로 소풍을 많

이 가요. 여름에는 덥고 비가 많이 와서 별로 좋지 않아요. 여름에는 근처에 있는 수영장에 수영하러 자주 가요. 시원한 가을에는 많은 사람들이 등산을 가요. 그러나, 한국의 겨울은 아주 춥고 눈도 많이 내려요. 겨울이 되면, 스키장에 스키타러 가요.

Key words

대체로	generally	수영장	swimming pool
분명하다	distinctive	등산가다	go mountain climbing
만발하다	in full blossom	내리다	fall down
소풍가다	go on a picnic	스키장	ski slope

16 외국인 숙소에서
At International House

> **By the end of this lesson you should be able to:**
> - talk about the place you are staying
> - make a phone call
> - use the indirect speech ending -고 하다
> - use the relative clause marker -ㄴ(은/는) 것
> - use the sentence ending -라고 하다
> - use the ㅂ, ㄹ irregular verbs

Dialogue 1 🔲🔲 *Samuel Kerry has taken a position as a CNN news reporter at the Korea branch in Seoul a couple of months ago and is staying at International House. Youngsik Lee, a Korean staffer, is curious to know about his new life at International House and asks him some somewhat personal questions*

영식: 언제부터 외국인 숙소에서 사셨어요?
쌤: 2개월 전부터 거기에서 살고 있어요.
영식: 그 숙소는 회사에서 가까워요?
쌤: 예, 아주 가까워서 걸어 다니고 있어요.
영식: 숙식비는 비싸요?
쌤: 사람들은 비싸다고 해요.
      독방을 쓰는데, 한달에 70만원이에요.
영식: 매우 비싸네요! 한국음식은 잘 드세요?
쌤: 매운 것은 잘 못 먹어요. 불고기는 아주 좋아요.
영식: 그럼, 다음에 제가 불고기 한번 살게요.
쌤: 좋습니다.

Vocabulary

숙소	living quarters	독방	single room
살다	live	한 달	one month

2개월 전	two months ago	70만원	700,000 won
회사	company	들다	eat (honorific)
걸어 다니다	walk	매운 것	hot things
숙식비	room and board	매우	very
한번	once	외국인	foreigner

Language points

The noun suffix -전부터

This suffix, when attached to the noun implying time, expresses "since," "ago," "before."

언제부터 한국어 배우기 시작했어요?	(Since) When did you begin to learn Korean?
어제부터 수영 배우기 시작했어요.	I began to learn swimming(since) yesterday.

The indirect speech ending -고 하다

This ending is used to report in an indirect way what someone has said. Declarative indirect speech is made by attaching the ending -고 하다 to the end of the quoted sentence. It is equivalent to the expression, "They say that . . ."

내 친구는 내일 러시아에 간다고 해요.	They say that one of my friends goes to Russia tomorrow.
내일은 날씨가 나쁘다고 해요.	They say that the weather will be bad tomorrow.
Peter는 한국 여자와 결혼했다고 해요.	They say that Peter married a Korean woman.

However, when the quoted sentence ends in linking verbs 이다/ 아니다, the indirect speech form -라고/아니라고 하다 is used to express the present tense.

그분은 장관이다.	He's a minister.
그분은 장관이라고 한다.	They say that he's a minister.
그것은 진짜 돈이 아니다.	It's not real money.
그것은 진짜 돈이 아니라고 한다.	They say that it's not real money.

The compound verb -다니다

This verb is combined with certain types of verb and indicates repetitive or ongoing action. Its literal meaning is "come around," "go around."

도서관에 걸어 다녀요.	I walk to the library.
회사까지 걸어 다녀요.	I walk to my company.
지하철역에서 집까지 걸어 다녀요.	I walk to my home from the subway station.

Irregular verbs ending in ㅂ

When a vowel follows, the final consonant ㅂ of the stem in some verbs changes into 우. *Note*: the inserted vowel 우 is contracted into the next vowel -어, yielding the syllable 워.

가볍다	light	→	가벼워요
덥다	warm	→	더워요
어둡다	dark	→	어두워요
가깝다	near	→	가까워요

The verbs 좋다 and 좋아하다

좋다 is an adjectival verb. It does not need an object after it. Since it is adjectival, the verb 좋다 can take the relative clause marker -ㄴ(은) to indicate the present tense. Its meaning is equivalent to English "good," "OK." The verb 좋아하다, on the other hand, is an action verb which does require an object. This verb can take the relative clause marker -는 for the present tense and -ㄴ(은) for the past tense. Its meaning is equivalent to "like" or "love."

내일은 날씨가 좋아요.	Tomorrow's weather is good.
뉴욕에는 좋은 식당이 있어요.	There are good restaurants in New York City.
Jane은 값이 비싼 청바지를 입어요.	Jane wears expensive jeans.
나는 머리가 긴 여자를 좋아해요.	I like a girl who has long hair.
나를 좋아하는 남학생이 점심을 사 주었다.	The male student who loves me bought me lunch.

Exercises

1 Someone compliments you on your excellent Korean. Tell him that you only started learning Korean two years ago.

2 A fellow swimmer at the pool compliments you on your technique. Tell her that you learned to swim ten years ago.

3 Someone asks you about Dong Woo's whereabouts. Tell him that you heard that Dong Woo:

a returned to America
b was sick
c disappeared

4 Someone at work asks how you get to the office every morning. Tell him that you get to work by walking, since your home is near the company's offices.

5 Correct your friend's grammar:

a 그는 사과를 좋다.
b 그 사람을 사과를 좋아한다.
c John은 한국이 좋아해서 한국 여자와 결혼했다.
d 그 여학생은 내가 좋은 학생이예요.

6 Someone asks you where you live. Tell him that you live:

a in an apartment near the company
b at International House
c at a relative's house

7 Someone wants to give you a big treat, and he asks you what kind of Korean food you like best. Tell him that you like Pulgogi best.

8 You have moved to a new place, and a friend asks you about it. Translate this dialogue into Korean:

A: Where do you live right now?
B: I live at the Hoam Faculty House.
A: Is it near the place where you work?
B: No, it's quite far away. So, I go to work by bus every morning.

9 Complete the following dialogue:

A:지금 어디에서 사세요?
B:

A: 숙식비는 비싸요?
B:
A: 한국 음식은 어때요?
B:
A: 무슨 음식을 가장 좋아 하세요?
B:
A: 그럼, 오늘 저녁에 내가 갈비 한 번 살게요.

Culture point

When a foreign traveler enters Seoul, he may wonder what major media services are available. There are two English language-based daily newspapers – the *Korea Times* and the *Korea Herald*, which are available at most newsstands and stores. You can usually get a copy of the *New York Times*, *Los Angeles Times*, *Chicago Tribune*, and London *Times* at the counter of major first-rate hotels. Korea has four TV networks, all broadcasting in Korean. These are KBS, MBC, SBS, and EBS. There is also the American Forces Korea Network (AFKN), which broadcasts exclusively in English on behalf of the U.S. military stationed throughout the country. AFKN's programs are not limited to military events: AFKN also broadcasts a diverse range of world news and sports 24 hours a day. Reception for AFKN is not always good outside Seoul.

You can find a public telephone on almost every street corner in Seoul. For a local call, deposit two Korean coins (₩10) for three minutes. But to make a long-distance call to Korean cities, you can use larger coins like the ₩50, ₩100, and ₩500. For an international call, check the country and area codes on the information sheet attached to the telephone booth and dial the numbers as directed. For example, when one wants to make a call to the U.S.A. one has to dial a series of numbers: 001 (or 002) – 1 – area code – phone number. To make an international call, it is convenient to use a telephone card, which one can purchase at designated places. Telephone cards are sold for ₩3,000, ₩5,000, and ₩10,000.

Dialogue 2 🔲 *Samuel Kerry returns from work to International House and asks the clerk whether he has received any phone messages for him*

쌤: 아저씨, 저한테 오늘 전화 온 것 있었어요?
아저씨: 예, 부산에 있는 친구한테서 전화 왔었어요.
쌤: 뭐라고 했어요?

아저씨: 저녁에 다시 (전화) 건다고 했어요.
　　　　그런데, 별로 급하지 않다고 했어요.
쌤:　　그래요?. 제가 먼저 전화를 해 봐야겠어요.
　　　　여보세요. 거기 부산이지요?
대화자: 예, 누굴 찾으세요?
쌤:　　저 민선이 친구인데, 있으면 바꿔 주세요.
대화자: 민선씨요? 여기에 그런 분 안 계시는데요.
쌤:　　거기가 333국의 7592번 아닙니까?
대화자: 예, 아니예요. 여기는 332국의 7592번이예요.
쌤:　　그래요? 전화 잘못 걸어서 미안합니다.

Vocabulary

전화	phone call	누굴(누구를)	whom
전화온것	phone call that came	바꿔주다	let me speak to
부산	Pusan	국	station number
한테서	from	번	number
저녁/밤	evening	잘못 걸다	dial the wrong number
전화걸다	make a phone call	미안하다	sorry
급하다	urgent	쌤	Sam

Language points

The relative clause marker - ㄴ(은/는) 것

This pattern is equivalent to the relative clauses "the one which . . . ,"
"that which . . . ," or "what . . ." as in the sentence "This is the one
which I lost in a train." The modifying phrase, placed before the
word 것 "thing," takes - ㄴ (은) for an adjectival verb (present tense)
and for action verbs (past tense). It also takes -는 for action verbs
(present tense).

제일 값이 싼 것을 사세요.	Please buy the cheapest one.
제일 모양이 좋은 것을 사세요.	Please buy the one which looks the best.
우리가 먹은 것은 너무 매워요.	What we had is too hot.
우리는 회장님이 말씀하시는 것을 노트에다 써요.	We write in a notebook what the chairman says.

The postposition -한테서

This is used to denote a person as the source or origin of an action. But for an inanimate source or origin the postposition -에서 is used.

오늘 아침에 친구한테서 　전화가 왔어요.	This morning a phone call 　came from my friend.
어머님한테서 편지가 왔어요.	A letter came from my 　mother.
편지가 집에서 왔어요.	A letter has come from my 　home.
전화가 고향에서 왔어요.	A phone call came from my 　hometown.

The sentence ending -라고 하다

This ending is attached to nouns of various types and indicates "This is (called) . . ." (*lit.* "This is being called as . . .").

이게 뭐예요?	What's this?
이것은 칠판이라고 해요.	We call this a blackboard.
저는 박상석이라고 해요.	I am Sang Seok Park.
이 단어는 한국어로 　뭐라고 해요?	What do you call this word in 　Korean?

The ㄹ irregular verb

Lesson 7 introduced some ㄹ irregular verbs which drop the consonant before the consonant ㅅ. The verb 걸다 also obeys this deletion rule when either ㄷ or ㅅ follows it.

전화 걸었어요.	I made a phone call.
전화를 건 사람은 　누구지요?	Who's the person that made a 　phone call?
전화를 건다고 했어요.	(He) said that he will make a 　phone call.

Answering negative questions in Korean

Special attention should be paid to the ways in which Koreans respond to a negative question. When they respond with "예," it means that what the speaker has asked is correct. However, when they respond "아니오" it means that what he/she has asked is incorrect i.e., conflicts with the answer.

오늘 저녁에 도서관에 가요?	Are you going to the library tonight?
예, 가요.	Yes, I am.
아니오, 가지 않아요.	No, I am not.
한국어 사전을 사지 못했어요?	Couldn't you buy a Korean dictionary?
예, 사지 못 했어요.	No, I couldn't.
지금 도서관에 안 가요?	Aren't you going to the library now?
아니오, 가요.	Yes, I am.

The contracted form 누굴

When the question word 누구 takes the object marker -을/를, only the consonant ㄹ is carried underneath the second syllable 구. This process yields the contraction 굴.

역에서 누구를 만났어요?	Who did you meet at the station?
역에서 누굴 만났어요?	Who did you meet at the station?

Korean telephone numbers

A typican Korean number consists of the station and individual telephone number (e.g., 496–3879). One can read these whole numbers as they are or the single digit numbers by using the Sino-Korean method. Note that the suffix -에 is inserted after the station number. It is equivalent to a dash (–) in English.

집 전화 번호가 몇 번이에요?	What's your home phone number?
사백구십육국에 삼천팔백칠십구번 입니다.	It's 496–3879.
사구육에 삽팔칠구번입니다.	It's 496–3879.

When you make a phone call from smaller local cities to Seoul, you have to dial "02" first, and then the rest of the numbers. You can find city codes for all other Korean cities in the telephone directory.

Exercises

10 Someone sees you reading a letter and asks you who it came from. Tell him that it came from your younger brother.

11 Someone sees you reading a letter and asks you where it came from. Tell him that the letter came from your home.

12 You do not know the Korean names of the objects you have in front of you. Ask what these words are in Korean:

a belt
b purse
c pocket-size notebook

13 Someone asks you whether you did the following, and you are sure that you didn't, or wouldn't, do them. How would you respond?

a 어제 교회에 갔어요?
b 지난 일요일에 Casino에 안 갔어요?
c 내일 한국 영화 보지 않겠어요?
d 육개장 안 먹어 봤어요?

14 You return to the guest house where you are staying and the clerk tells you there was a phone call for you. Ask him the name of the person who called you.

15 A Korean businessman treats you to an excellent meal. He asks you how you liked the food. Tell him that what you had was delicious.

16 You are holding a staff meeting, and you think that it's a good idea for staff members to write down what you say. How do you tell them to do so?

17 You dial the telephone number for your friend's house, and you are told that you have dialed the wrong number. How do you apologize to the person answering the phone?

18 You answer the phone, and the person at the other end of the line wants to speak with someone you do not know. How can you tell the person that he has the wrong number?

19 Translate the following dialogue into Korean:

A: Is there a phone message for me?
B: Yes, a guy from KBS called you.
A: Do you have his phone number?

B: Here it is.
A: I must call him right away.
B: It's aready seven o'clock. He must have left work for the day.
A: You're right. I'll call him tomorrow morning.

20 Complete the following dialogue:

A: 여보세요? 거기에 김문수씨 계세요?
B:
A: 거기가 653에 3546번 아닙니까?
B:
A: 아, 알겠습니다. 미안합니다.

21 Reading passage ▣▣ Samuel Kerry took a job as a CNN
news reporter in Seoul and arrived at Kimport Airport on a humid
summer day. He took a taxi and checked into International House.
However, it took him more than two hours because he had a couple of problems. Try to figure out what problems he ran into and
how he overcame them.

Samuel Kerry는 CNN 방송국 기자로 서울지국에 부임하게 되었다. 어
느 더운 여름날 그는 김포공항에 도착한 후에, 택시를 타고 외국
인 숙소까지 갔다. 가는데 교통이 너무 밀려서, 택시가 빨리 달릴
수가 없었다. 또한, 택시 운전사는 Kerry씨의 영어 발음을 잘못 알
아 듣고, Intercontinental Hotel에 내려 주었다. 거기에 있는 경비원
아저씨의 도움을 받아, 다시 택시를 타고 외국인 숙소로 갈 수
있었다. 그러나, 공항에서 숙소까지 3시간이 넘게 걸렸다.

Key words

방송국	broadcast station	교통	traffic
기자	reporter	발음	pronunciation
지국	branch bureau	경비원	guard
부임하다	take a new position (job)		

17 한국집에 초대받기
Invitation to a Korean house

By the end of this lesson you should be able to:
- accept an invation to a Korean home
- express likes and dislikes
- use the nominalizing marker -기
- use the sentence endings -(으)면 좋겠다, 아(어/여)도 되다, -ㄴ(는)편이다
- use the conjunctions -만, ㄹ(을)때에
- use the ㅎ irregular verbs
- use the sentence ending -어 보이다

Dialogue 1 ▩▩ *Mr. Kim, section chief of a trading company, invites several of his staff members, including Ms. Jones, to a party. She works as copy editor for the English section of the company's magazine. Since she is not familiar with Seoul streets, he gives Ms. Jones a hand-sketched map of the area near his house*

김: 존스 선생님, 이번 주말에 저의 집에서 파티하는데 오실
      수 있어요?
존스: 아, 그러세요? 그런데, 그 날이 무슨 날이에요?
김: 아뇨, 아무 날도 아닙니다.
      그저 회사 직원들을 초대해서 저녁을 대접할까 합니다.
존스: 몇시에 갈까요?
김: 저녁 6시에 오세요.
존스: 김과장님댁 주소는 어떻게 되지요?
김: 네, 한남동 185번지입니다.
존스: 한국집은 찾기가 힘들어요. 약도 있으면 좋겠어요.
김: 맞아요. 약도하고 주소 여기 있습니다.
      (약도를 보면서) 우체국에서 저의 집이 보입니다.
존스: 찾아갈 수 있을 것 같아요.

Vocabulary

주말	weekend	댁	hourse (honorific)
파티하다	throw a party	주소	address
무슨 날	what kind of date	한남동	Hannam-Dong
아무날도	no particular date	번지	street number
직원	staff	약도	sketched map
초대하다	invite	우체국	post office
과장님	section chief	대접하다	treat

Language points

The sentence ending -(으)면 좋겠다

This ending is used to express a speaker's wish for something to happen or be done to his or her advantage. Its meaning is equivalent to the expression "I wish/hope . . ."

비가 안 오면 좋겠다.	I hope it won't rain.
사람들이 파티에 많이 오면 좋겠다.	I hope a lot of people come to the party.
돈이 많이 있으면 좋겠다.	I wish I had a lot of money.

The nominalizing marker -기

Lesson 15 introduced two uses for the nominalizing suffix -기. In the third kind, when it is attached to the verb stem, this marker converts action verbs into the verbal noun forms "-ing," "to do something." This changed form can take a subject or object case marker in a sentence.

공부하다	study	→	공부하기	studying
달리다	run	→	달리기	running
읽다	read	→	읽기	reading

시험 공부하기가 쉽지 않아요.	It's not easy studying for the test.
그는 어제부터 시험 공부를 시작했어요.	He began studying for the test (since) yesterday.
내 동생은 책 읽기를 좋아해요.	My younger brother likes reading books.

The verbs 보다/보이다

보다 is an active verb which is usually used when a speaker intends a voluntary action ("look at", or "watch"). In this usage, the object case marker (-을/를) can be taken. But 보이다 is the passive form of a verb used for his or her involuntary state of being "visible." In this case, the subject case marker (-이/가) can be recovered.

어제 회사에서 Jane 봤어요?	Did you see Jane at the company yesterday?
저 큰 건물(을) 보세요.	Look at the big building over there.
저 큰 건물(이) 보입니까?	Can you see the big building over there?

Exercises

1 A friend of yours asks you what you hope for in the New Year. Tell him that you want three things:

a to become richer
b to be promoted
c to take a round-the-world trip

2 Imagine that you have recently been relocated to a Seoul office. Your supervisor wants to know what kinds of problems you are facing in your new life in Seoul. Tell her that it is difficult to do the following things:

a take a taxi
b have a good night's sleep
c find American food

3 Mr. Lee, section chief in your office, asks you whether you can come to a party this coming Saturday. How do you accept his offer?

4 When you are invited to a party by Mr. Lee, you don't know the area where he lives. Tell him that you need a sketched map.

5 You have an appointment with a Korean businessman, and you've had detailed directions from him over the phone. Tell him that you are confident you'll find his place.

6 Correct your friend's grammar:

a 저기에 빨간 건물이 봐요.

b 저기 있는 큰 건물을 보여요.

c 큰. 건물이 ·보는 쪽에서 우리 집은 왼쪽에 있습니다.

7 Translate the following dialogue into Korean:

A: What are you going to do over the weekend?

B: I'm free.

A: Can you come over to my house?

B: Is it a special day?

A: No, I just want to spend (some) time with you.

8 Complete the following dialogue:

A: 오늘 저녁에 뭐 하세요?

B:

A: 선약이 없으면, 우리 집에 가서 맥주 한 잔 .해요.

B:

A: 그럼, 내일 저녁은 어때요?

B:

A: 내일 일이 끝난 후에 지하 다방에서 만나요.

B:

Culture point

When a foreigner works at a Korean or American company in Korea
for any period of time, the chances are that he or she is likely to be
invited to a Korean home at some time or another. When such a
visit occurs, it is quite acceptable/normal to bring the host(ess) some
type of gift. But a foreigner may be surprised that the host(ess) does
not unwrap the gift or make any comment on it in front of him or
her. One reason for this behavior is that many Koreans do not like
looking frivolous by revealing what the gift is to others who may be
around at the time when it is given. Their attitude is that only a *child*
gets a gift from a giver, opens it, and then uses it at once. The
Confucian tradition trains Koreans to aspire to look very reserved,
respectful, calm, even if there is something that is distracting them.
Another possible reason is the concept of face-saving. At the moment
when the gift is being opened, the recipient may unconsciously indicate that the gift is somehow not suitable. In this case, the host or
hostess's attitude might make the visitor feel uncomfortable – and
thus "face" would be lost. A foreigner should, therefore, not feel
embarrassed when a Korean host accepts a gift and puts it away
somewhere on a shelf.

Dialogue 2 **CD** *Ms. Jones arrives at Kim's house and hands him a small gift. At the party Ms. Jones compliments him on the variety of tasty-looking food on offer*

김: 죤스 선생님, 어서 오세요.
죤스: 예. 김과장님, 여기 조그만 선물 가져 왔습니다.
김: 아이구, 그냥 오셔도 되는데요.
죤스: 별거 아닙니다.
김: 차린 것은 변변치 않습니다만, 많이 드세요.
죤스: 차린 음식들이 너무 맛있어 보입니다.
김: 칭찬해 주셔서 감사합니다. 죤스 선생님, 매운 반찬 잘 드세요?
죤스: 잘 먹는 편이에요.
　　　김치가 맵지만, 먹을 때에 찬물을 많이 마시면 되거든요.
김: 야, 죤스 선생님은 머리가 비상하네요!
죤스: 아니예요. 제 친구가 가르쳐 주었어요.

Vocabulary

조그만	tiny		매운 반찬	hot side-dishes
선물	gift		가져오다	bring
아이구	oh!		변변치 않다	not good
그냥	just		편	side
별거	not that		김치	Kimchi
차린 것	things that one displayed		맵다	hot and spicy
			물	water
맛	taste		비상한	extremely smart
칭찬하다	praise		가르쳐 주다	teach

Language points

The ㅎ irregular verbs

Some adjectival verbs conjugate irregularly, in that the final consonant ㅎ of the stem is subject to deletion before such consonants as ㄴ,ㄹ,ㅁ and the vowel ㅇ.

빨갛다	red	→	빨간
하얗다	white	→	하얀
노랗다	yellow	→	노란
조그맣다	tiny	→	조그만
이렇다	be like this	→	이런

The permissive sentence ending
-아(어/여)도 되다

This ending is used to express the concession "may." Other words, such as 좋다 or 괜찮다 can follow -도. They mean either "it's all right" or "it doesn't matter."

회의에 늦게 와도 됩니다. It's all right even if you are late
　　　　　　　　　　　　　for the meeting.
내일 다시 와도 됩니다. It's all right even if you come
　　　　　　　　　　　　　again tomorrow.
그 일을 내일 해도 돼요. You may do that work tomorrow.

Another contrastive conjunction -만

Lessons 8 and 10 introduced two kinds of contrastive conjunctions -지만 and -(으)나. This conjunction is attached to a clause ending in -니다 and means "although" or "but." The second conjunction tends to be more formal than the first one.

그 분이 회의에 오셨습니다만, 만나지 못 했습니다.
Although he came to the meeting, I couldn't meet him.

교통사고가 났습니다만, 운전사는 다치지 않았습니다.
Although the traffic accident took place, the driver did not get hurt.

The sentence ending -어 보이다

This ending is attached to the stem of adjectival verbs and means "seem" + adjective.

그 사람은 키가 커 보입니다. He seems tall.
그 음식은 아주 매워 보입니다. The food seems very hot and
　　　　　　　　　　　　　　　spicy.

The temporal conjunction - ㄹ/을 때에

This conjunction is used with any verbs and indicates adverbial expressions of time. Its meaning is equivalent to "at the time when . . ."

학교에 올 때에 책을 　가져 오세요.	Please bring your book when 　you come to school.
날씨가 좋을 때 공원에 　갑시다.	Let's go to the park if (when) 　the weather is good.
물건 값이 비쌀 때는 　사지 맙시다.	Let's not buy it if (when) the 　merchandise is expensive.

Note: This conjunction can also take such particles as -가/이, -를/을, -도, -부터.

공부할 때가 되었어요.	It's time to study.
봄에 눈이 올 때도 있었어요.	At times, it snowed in the spring.

The sentence ending - ㄴ(는) 편이다

This sentence ending is used with any verb and indicates one's habitual action in doing something when we want to distinguish between what one can do and what one cannot do. Thus, it is equivalent to ". . . can do something well."

Peter씨는 매운 음식을 잘 먹는 편이다.
Peter can eat hot and spicy food well.

나는 한국에 오랫동안 살았는데도, 한국음식을 잘 못 먹는 편이에요.
Although I lived in Korea for a long time, I can't eat Korean food well.

Exercises

9 At the doorstep of Mr. Kim's house, you hand him a gift. As a matter of courtesy, you want to tell him that it is only small. What would you say?

10 You have invited Mr. Kim to your house for a year-end party. He calls you to tell you that he is going to be late because of a traffic jam. Tell him that it's all right to come a bit late.

11 You are led to a table full of good food. You want to compliment the hostess on her excellent cooking skills by saying that all of the food looks tasty. What would you say?

12 You have borrowed a Korean dictionary from a friend, and he tells you that he needs it back. Tell him that you are going to return it to him when you see him tomorrow.

13 At a party, one of the guests asks you whether you like eating Korean food. Tell him that you do.

14 Rearrange the words of the following dialogue to make sense:

A: 참석하지, 사장님은, 회의에, 출근했지만, 않았다
B: 맛, 음식이, 보인다, 차린, 있어
A: 맵지만, 김치가, 잘, 먹는, 저는, 편이에요.
B: 물을, 마셔요, 많이, 김치를, 매운, 먹을 때는

15 Translate the following dialogue into Korean:

A: Which Korean food do you like best?
B: I like something that is not too hot.
A: Do you like Chapchae?
B: Of course I do.
A: How about Kimchi?
B: I don't like Kimchi too much, because it is so hot.

16 Complete the following dialogue:

A: 어제 어디 갔어요?
B:
A: 무슨 날이었어요?
B:
A: 홍과장님 댁에서 한국음식 많이 먹었어요?
B:
A: 무슨 음식이 가장 맛이 있었어요?
B:
A: 저는 채식을 하기 때문에, 불고기는 잘 안 먹어요.

17 *Reading passage* One Saturday evening James Goldsmith is invited to Mr. Lee's house for a social gathering of the staff in his office. On his way to Mr. Kim's house, he drops into a flower shop and buys a dozen roses as a gift for Mr. Kim's wife. When he arrives at Mr. Kim's house on time, he is taken by surprise to find that no one else is there. Try to figure out how James has gone wrong and how he overcomes his problem.

어느 토요일 저녁에 James Goldsmith씨는 김과장님 댁에 초대 받았다. 김과장님 댁에 가는 길에 꽃가게에 들러서 사모님께 주려고 장미 한 다발을 샀다. 선물을 가지고 6시에 김과장님 댁에 도착했을 때 손님들이 없었다. 이상해서 김과장님께 물어 봤을 때, 손님들이 7시에 온다고 했다. 그때부터 둘이는 손님들이 올 때까지 비디오 영화를 봤다. 7시에 회사 직원 손님들이 전부 와서, 그때부터 재미 있는 파티가 시작되었다.

Key words

초대받다	be invited	한 다발	one bunch
꽃가게	flower shop	이상한	strange
들리다	drop by	비디오	videotape
사모님	honorific word referring to someone's wife		

18 이사하기
Moving

By the end of this lesson you should be able to:
- talk about moving into a Korean apartment
- use the sentence endings -면서요?, ㄴ(은) 모양이다,
  -곤 하다, ㄹ(을) 계획이다
- use the sentence endings -ㄹ(을) 필요가 있다, ㄴ(은)지가…되다
- use the conjunctions -자마자, ㄹ(을)겸
- use the sentence ending -ㄹ(을) 시간이 있다

Dialogue 1   *John Armstrong has recently moved into a new apartment. Mr. Chang, a colleague, asks him about it*

장: 새 아파트로 이사했다면서요?

암스트롱: 예, 한 달 전에 이사했어요.

장: 평수가 어떻게 됩니까?

암스트롱: 30평인데 서민 아파트입니다.

장: 암스트롱씨, 돈을 많이 번 모양이군요.

암스트롱: 아니오. 회사에서 무료로 임대 해 준 거예요.

장: 동네 사람들은 만나 봤어요?

암스트롱: 예, 이사하자마자 옆집 사람들을 초대해서 한 턱 냈어요.

장: 동네는 조용합니까?

암스트롱: 아뇨. 때로는 밤 늦게까지 소란스러운 때도 있어요.

장: 저희 동네도 마찬가지에요.
여름에는 밤 12시까지 차 소리가 나곤 해요.

Vocabulary

아파트	apartment	동네	neighborhood
이사하다	move	옆집	next door
평수	Pyong	한 턱 내다	give a treat
	(= 3.954 square yards)		

서민 아파트	apartment units for low-income people	소리가 나다	make noise
암스트롱씨	Mr. Armstrong	벌다	earn
모양이다	it seems ...	조용하다	quiet
무료로	for free	때로는.	at times
임대해주다	rent a property (for an employee)	밤 늦게까지	until late at night
		소란스럽다	boisterous
		마찬가지다	same

Language points

The sentence ending -면서요?

This interrogative ending, when attached to the declarative ending (-다) of a sentence, is used to ask a listener to confirm knowledge about a certain fact or event which a speaker has acquired from someone or a public source (e.g., the media).

그 사람 영국에 갔다면서요?
I heard that he went to England. Is it true?

어제 동대문 시장에서 불이 났다면서요?
I heard that a fire broke out at the Dongdaemoon market yesterday. Is it true?

However, when the sentence ends with a linking verb (or verbs) (-이다/아니다), the last syllable of the verb changes to -라, to which the different ending -면서요? is attached.

| 저분이 회사 사장님이라면서요? | They say that he is a president of the company, am I right? |
| 저 건물은 67층이라면서요? | They say that building has 67 stories, am I right? |

The sentence ending -ㄴ(은) 모양이다

This ending is attached to the stem of the action verb and indicates the likelihood that some event has happened. Its meaning is equivalent to "it seems to be ...," "it looks like ...," or "it seems as if ..." It may take other suffixes (ㄴ/은,는,ㄹ/을) to express, respectively, the present tense for an adjectival verb, the present tense for an action verb, and the future tense for an action verb:

내 친구는 어제 회의에 늦게 온 모양입니다.
It seems that my friend was late for the meeting yesterday.

차가 고속도로에서 고장난 모양입니다.
It seems that the car was broken down on the highway.

요즈음 차 값이 싼 모양이에요.
These days, it seems that cars are inexpensive.

학생들이 아직도 복도에서 기다리는 모양입니다.
It seems that students are still waiting in the hall.

이번에 김 과장은 비싼 차를 살 모양입니다.
It seems that Section Chief Kim will buy an expensive car.

The conjunction -자마자

This conjunction is used to express one action that is immediately followed by another. It is equivalent to various English expressions ("as soon as . . . ," "no sooner . . . than . . . ," "immediately after . . . ," etc.).

학교에 가자마자 도서관에 갔어요.
As soon as I went to school, I went to the library.

도서관이 열자마자 학생들이 떼지어 들어갔다.
As soon as the library was open, students rushed in in groups.

The sentence ending -곤 하다

This ending is attached to the stem of an action verb and expresses a speaker's repetitive action in the present tense. It is equivalent to the English words "often," "occasionally," "frequently." Note that the tense is reflected in the verb 하다.

John은 일요일도 회사에 나가곤 해요.
John often goes to work, even on Sundays.

4월에도 눈이 많이 오곤 해요.
It often snows a lot, even in April.

Armstrong씨는 미국에 있을 때, 무역회사에서 일하곤 했어요.
When he was in America, Mr. Armstrong used to work for the
trading company.

The compound verb 한 턱 내다

This verb means "give one a big treat." You may hear this type
of expression very often once you start working with Korean colleagues.

새로 이사했으니까,	Because I moved (home), I'll
한 턱 내야지요.	have to give you a big treat.
다음 달에 승진하면	When I'm promoted next
한 턱 내겠어요.	month, I'll given you a big treat.

The expression 마찬가지다

This expression is used to reflect what a speaker has already said
and is equivalent to "much the same."

오늘 비가 많이 왔어요.	Today it rained a lot.
내일도 마찬가지예요.	It's (going to be) much the same tomorrow.
요즈음 수박 값이 비싸요.	These days, watermelon is expensive.
참외 값도 마찬가지예요.	Melon is much the same.

Exercises

1 You have heard that Mr. Armstrong recently moved to a new
apartment, and you want to make sure this is true. What would
you ask him?

2 While you are riding in a taxi, you notice a high tower-block to
your left. You remember having heard that it's a 46-story building. Ask the driver whether that's true.

3 A friend of yours has bought a new apartment as well as a new
car. He seems to have made a fortune. How might you comment
on it?

4 A colleague is looking for Mr. Chang, and you saw him go out a minute ago. Tell your colleague that Mr. Chang went out as soon as the meeting was over.

5 You are being interviewed for a receptionist job, and the interviewer asks about your work experience. Tell him that you used to be a secretary at City Hall.

6 Someone asks what you spend time doing at weekends. Tell him that you frequently go climbing with a group of friends.

7 You have moved to a new apartment and you think that it would be a good idea to invite your office colleagues to a celebratory party. Tell them that you would like to give them a big treat.

8 A friend tells you that the outside of the apartment where she lives is very noisy up until 10 P.M. Your place is much the same. What would you say?

9 Correct your friend's grammar:

a Jane은 다음 달에 일본에 간 모양이에요.
b 내 동생은 집에 온자마자 화장실에 들어갔다.
c 여름에 날씨가 더우면, 사람들은 옷이 벗곤한다.

10 Translate the following dialogue into Korean:

A: I heard that you've moved to an expensive apartment. Is this true?
B: Yeah. It's three months since I moved in.
A: How big is it?
B: It's about 25 Pyong. It's OK for the three of us in our family.
A: Have you met any people in the apartment complex?
B: Not yet. But I'm going to invite a group of people for a getting-to-know-you party.
A: When you do, please invite me as well!
B: Of course!

11 Complete the dialogue:

A: 언제 새 아파트로 이사 갔어요?
B:
A: 아파트 주민들은 만났어요?
B:
A: 그럼, 한번 사람들을 초대해서 한 턱 내야지요.
B:
A: 빨리 하면 좋아요.
B:

Culture point
Most Korean citizens live in apartments in an apartment complex. Mammoth apartment complexes cluster around Seoul. Even a tiny-looking apartment cell (equivalent to approx. 100 sq. feet) costs $100,000 (equivalent to 25 Pyong), so many Koreans buy a smaller apartment unit and then move to a bigger unit as the household income increases. Koreans have not adopted a rental system for apartments, as Americans and British people have. They usually buy an apartment, small or big, depending on its affordability. In this case, middle-class Koreans can borrow 20 percent of the full cost from their bank. They usually pay the remaining amount as a cash down-payment. In many instances, buyers may end up borrowing a large amount from family members or close friends, unless they are rich enough to pay for their apartments entirely in cash. There are still many traditional Korean houses, which older people seem to prefer to live in. The price of these houses is a bit lower than those of modern apartments in an apartment complex, where a whole range of facilities, ranging from cleaners to drugstores, are within walking distance.

Dialogue 2 🔲🔲 *A colleague asks Mr. Armstrong about the new apartment he's recently moved into. Mr. Armstrong says that it is messy and the furniture needs to be arranged properly*

김: 새로 이사간 아파트의 짐 정리는 다 되었어요?
암스트롱: 아니오. 짐이 다 정리되지 않아서 엉망입니다.
김: 가구도 새로 사셨어요?
암스트롱: 아직 살 시간이 없었어요.
내일 집사람과 같이 나가서 살 계획입니다.
김: 방은 몇 개나 돼요?
암스트롱: 온돌방이 둘 있고, 응접실이 하나 있어요.
김: 소파와 찬장은 살 필요가 없어요?
암스트롱: 그것들은 산 지가 얼마되지 않아서 아직도 깨끗해요.
집이 정리되면, 구경할 겸해서 놀러 오세요.
김: 시간나면 한번 놀러 갈게요.

Vocabulary

짐	moving stuff	응접실	living room
정리되다	in order	찬장	cupboard

엉망이다	messy	소파	sofa
·새로운	new	필요	need (noun)
가구	furniture	아직도	yet
살 시간	time to buy	깨끗하다	clean
집사람	one's wife	시간나다	have time
계획	plan	구경하다	look around

Language points

The sentence ending - ㄹ(을) 시간이 있다

This ending is attached to the stem of any action verb and indicates that a speaker has time to do something. 없다 replaces 있다 to express "no time to do something."

오후에 회의할 시간이 있어요.
I have time to attend the meeting in the afternoon.

바빠서 책 읽을 시간이 없어요.
Because I'm busy, I don't have time to read books.

일요일에도 등산할 시간이 없어요.
I don't have time to climb, not even on Sundays.

The sentence ending - ㄹ(을) 계획이다

This ending is attached to the stem of any action verb and indicates that a speaker has a plan to do something.

주말에 부산에 갈 계획입니다.
I'm planning to go to Pusan over the weekend.

다음 달에 새 아파트로 이사할 계획입니다.
I'm planning to move to a new apartment next month.

The sentence ending - ㄹ(을) 필요가 있다

This ending is attached to the stem of any action verb and indicates one's need to do something. The English equivalent is "one needs to do . . ." The case marker 가 is optional. The opposite meaning can be obtained by substituting 있다 with 없다.

시험 때는 공부를 많이 할 필요(가) 있어요.	I need to study a lot when I have a test.
피곤할 때는 잠을 많이 잘 필요(가) 있어요.	I need to sleep a lot when I am tired.

The sentence ending - ㄴ(은)지가...되다

This ending is used to express the time lapse in a noun clause ("It is ... since a certain action started."). The noun clause, which forms the first part of this ending, is always used as the subject of a sentence and is followed by the predicate, which specifies the length of time.

한국에 오신지(가) 몇 개월 됐어요?	How many months is it since you came to Korea?
새 집으로 이사한지(가) 일년 되었어요.	It's one year since I moved to my new house.
한국말을 공부한지(가) 2년이 됩니다.	It's two years since I studied (the) Korean (language).

The conjunction - ㄹ(을) 겸

This is used to express the idea of one action accompanying another at the same time ("to engage in two activities at the same time.").

물도 마실 겸, 차에서 내립시다.
Let's get out of the car and drink water.

시내 구경도 할 겸, 종로에 나갑시다.
Let's go out to Chongro and tour around downtown.

The noun 겸 may also be used to put two nouns in a row.

이 건물은 사무실 겸 주택이에요.
This building is used as both an office and living quarters.

The verb 겸하다 means to hold more than one job at the same time.

그 분은 과장을 겸하고 있습니다.
He is acting section chief (i.e., in addition to his original job).

Exercises

12 Mr. Lee, section chief of the office, wants to arrange a picnic for this coming Saturday. He asks you whether you have anything to do this weekend. Tell him politely that you have no time to go on a picnic.

13 A friend of yours wants to go shopping at Midopa (one of the old and best department stores in Seoul) with you, and you have a previous engagement. Tell her that you don't have time to go shopping.

14 Everyone in the office knows that the car you drive frequently breaks down, and a colleague wonders if you need a new car. Tell her that you plan to buy a new one.

15 You have moved to a new house, and someone asks you whether you need new furniture. Tell him that you have furniture that still looks brand new.

16 Mr. Lee wonders if he should attend a staff meeting for a certain project, and you think that he doesn't have to. Tell him that he does not have to attend the meeting this time.

17 You recently moved to a new condominium. You haven't let everyone in the office know this. Miss Lee, who *has* heard about it, asks you when you moved. Tell her that it's a year since you moved to your new apartment.

18 You want to persuade a friend to go to Myongdong (one of the busiest shopping streets in the eastern part of Seoul). He is not convinced. Tell him that you can catch a movie and at the same time do some shopping at the department store.

19 Translate the following dialogue into Korean:

A: How long is it since you moved (to a new house) in Kangnam?
B: It's about three months.
A: Everything in your house is all in order?
B: No, it's still messy.
A: Show me your house when it's ready.
B: Sure, I'd be glad to.

20 Complete the dialogue:

A: 집 정돈 다 됐어요?
B:

A: 그럼, 언제 정돈이 다 끝나지요?
B:
A: 다 정돈되면 회사 사람들 초대할거예요?
B:

21 Reading passage 🔲🔲 William Ryan, a news reporter, has bought a spacious new apartment in Kangnam, in the southern part of Seoul, and moved into it over a month ago. Colleagues in the office helped him move. Although Mr. Ryan has a plan to invite his colleagues to his apartment for a party, he thinks that he is not ready yet. When reading the passage, try to figure out how big his apartment is and why he is not ready to invite his colleagues.

William Ryan씨는 최근에 40평짜리 아파트를 사서 강남으로 이사 갔다. 지난 달 일요일에 회사 친구들이 이사를 도와 주었다. 이사 한 지가 한달이 넘었는데, 집은 아직 엉망이다. 다음 주에는 응접 실 가구와 소파 세트를 사려고 가구점에 갈 계획이다. 집 정돈이 끝나면 이사를 도와 준 회사 직원들을 초대해서 한 턱 내려고 한 다.

Key words

최근에	recently	엉망이다	(all) messy
강남	Kangnam ("south of Han river")	가구점	furniture store
		정돈	arrangements
이사가다	move	한 턱 내다	give (one) a (big) treat
한달이 넘다	over one month		

19 주유소에서
At the gas station

By the end of this lesson you should be able to:
- buy gas at a gas station
- have a car repaired at a service station
- use the sentence endings -ㄹ(을)뻔하다, -거든요, 아(어/여) 버리다, -기로 하다, -기는 하다, -(으)면 안되다
- use the conjunctions -(이) 라서, 동안에

Dialogue 1 ▢▢ *Sandra Hopkins is driving Su Jin Kwon along the bank of a river to find a suitable picnic spot. Sandra happens to notice that the gas is running dangerously low. They look for a gas station nearby and fill the car full of unleaded gasoline*

쌘드라:	가스가 거의 다 떨어지고 있는 것 같아요.
수진:	그래요. 이 근처는 농장이라서 주유소가 없는데요.
쌘드라:	그럼, 어디로 가야지요?
수진:	저기 길 모퉁이 보이죠?
	거기 지나서 좀 가면, 새로 생긴 주유소가 있을지 몰라요.
쌘드라:	한번 그리 가 봅시다.
수진:	아, 저기 새마을 주유소가 보이네요!
쌘드라:	나도 봤어요. 큰 일 날 뻔 했어요.
	(주유소에서)
종업원:	어서 오세요. 무엇을 도와 드릴까요?
쌘드라:	무연휘발유 4리터만 넣어 주세요.
종업원:	예, 예. 창문 청소는 안 하십니까?
쌘드라:	안해도 돼요. 아직도 깨끗하거든요.

Vocabulary

가스	gas	새마을 주유소	New Village Station
거의	almost		

떨어지다	run out	큰 일	big problem
농장	farm	도와 드리다	help someone
주유소	gas station	무연휘발유	unleaded gasoline
길모퉁이	corner	리터	liter
새로 생긴	newly opened	창문	window
근처	vicinity	청소	cleaning

Language points

The causal conjunction -(이) 라서

A few conjunctions used to combine a cause clause with an effect clause have been introduced already. These are 아(어/여)서 in Lesson 3, -(으)니까 in Lesson 12, and -기 때문에 in Lesson 13. However, *this* conjunction is directly attached only to nouns.

방학이라서 도서관에 학생들이 없어요.
Because it's a vacation, there are no students in the library.

조그만 가게라서 수입이 많지 않아요.
Because it is tiny, the gross income of the store isn't that big.

The sentence ending - ㄹ(을) 뻔 하다

This ending is used to indicate that a certain action has nearly taken place, but did not actually happen for some reason. The tense is shown on the end of the verb phrase. Its English equivalent is "to come close to doing/happening."

너무 늦게 일어나서 회의에 늦을 뻔 했다.
Because I woke up late, I was almost late for the meeting.

가스가 다 떨어져서 큰일 날 뻔 했다.
Because (my car) ran out of gas, I almost had a serious problem.

The compound verb form -아(어/여)주다

The verb 주다 can be combined with certain action verbs and implies that a speaker renders some service to the hearer. This compound verb is used when the speaker requests some service to be rendered or when he or she personally provides the service to the hearer who is lower in social rank and younger in age.

읽다 read → 읽어 주다 read for someone
가스를 넣다 put in gas → 가스를 넣어 주다 put in gas for someone
그 아이한테 책을 읽어 주세요. Read the book for that child.

The semi-causal sentence ending -거든요

This ending, when attached to any verb, provides a slight cause for the sentence immediately preceding the one containing the verb.

주말에 여행 못 갔어요. 비가 많이 왔거든요.
I didn't take a trip. It's because it rained a lot.

저녁에 도서관에 안 갈거에요. 피곤하거든요.
I'm not going to the library. It's because I'm tired.

Exercises

1 A friend asks why he didn't see you last week. Tell him that, since you were on vacation last week, you didn't come to work.

2 You and a friend of yours are out on the beach to beat the summer heatwave. Your friend is very surprised to see tens of thousands of people swarming along the seafront. Tell him that, because of the hot summer, a lot of people have come to the beach.

3 You overslept one morning. Later, one of your colleagues asks you how your morning was. Tell her that you were almost late for a meeting.

4 At a gas station an attendant asks you how much gas is left in the tank. Tell him there's almost none and you almost ran into a serious problem.

5 At a gas station, an attendant asks you how much gas you want to buy. Ask him for four liters.

6 A group of people in the office went on a picnic last Sunday, and you missed it. Monday morning, someone asks you why you didn't come. Tell him that you were sick.

7 A friend of yours compliments you on the pretty dress you are wearing. Tell him that it's a brand-new dress.

8 Translate the following dialogue into Korean:

A: Do you need gas?
B: Yes, I do. Please put in 2 liters.
A: No problem. Do you want your windshield wiped?
B: No, I don't think so, because I cleaned it this morning.
A: Oh, I see.

9 Complete the dialogue:

A: 기름이 다 떨어진 것 같은데요.
B:
A: 모르겠어요.
B:
A: 저기 경찰 아저씨는 알거예요.
B:
C: 저는 경찰이 아니예요. 군인이에요.
A and B:

Culture point

It is generally no problem for a first-time visitor to Korea to cope with the public transport systems. But you can choose to rent a car. However, many foreigners are reluctant to drive even a rental car because the traffic laws are different and visitors are not familiar with the roads. To rent a car, you should meet the following three requirements: 1, have an international driver's license with at least one year's experience; 2, be over 21 years old; 3, have a valid passport. It is customary for visitors who wish to hire a personal driver to pay his meals and hotel expenses. The cost of hiring a driver in Seoul is as high as w50,000 for 10 hours' service a day. One can obtain detailed information about car-rental service in major Korean cities by contacting the rental agencies themselves.

Dialogue 2 🔲 *Sandra and Su-Jin were enjoying a sunny afternoon lying on the grass. Suddenly it clouded over, so they packed their things and hurried to their car. On the way back home, Sandra thought that the car was not running too well. So, they pulled the car over for a checkup at the repair shop*

쌘드라: 여보세요. 제 차가 고장이 난 것 같은데 한번 봐 주시겠어요?
정비원: 테스트를 한번 해 보도록 하죠.

쌘드라: 아까 달리는데 이상한 소리가 나기는 했어요.
정비원: 라지에타에서 물이 새는 것 같군요.
쌘드라: 물이 샜어요?
정비원: 예, 라지에타 물이 다 빠져 버렸군요.
쌘드라: 아저씨, 빨리 고칠 수 없어요?
정비원: 글쎄요. 적어도 세 시간은 걸리겠는데요.
수진: 더 빨리 안 되겠어요?
　　　 저희들은 두 시간 후에 친구를 만나기로 했거든요.
정비원: 그럼, 두 시간 후에 오세요. 그 전에 오면 안 돼요.
쌘드라: 고치는 동안에 저기 찻집에 있을거에요.
　　　 정비 끝나면, 연락 주세요.

Vocabulary

쌘드라	Sandra	후에	after
고장이 나다	broken down	새다	leak out
봐주다	check	빠지다	drain out
테스트	test	고치다	fix
아까	a while ago	적어도	at least
이상한	strange	동안에	during
라지에타	radiator	찻집	tearoom
만나다	meet	정비	repair

Language points

The sentence ending -아(어/여) 버리다

This ending is used to express the completion or the exhaustion of a certain event by a verb in use. It translates as "to finish up doing something."

이 일을 한시간 내에 끝내 버립시다.	Let's finish (up) this work within an hour.
편지를 읽고 찢어 버렸어요.	I read the letter and tore it up.

The sentence ending -기로 하다

This ending is used to express a speaker's decision or agreement with himself or another person in a certain context. It is equivalent to "agree to" or "decide to."

두시에 친구하고 회사 앞에서 만나기로 했습니다.
I agreed to meet my friend at 2 P.M. in front of the company.

내일 저녁에는 도서관에 안 가기로 했습니다.
I decided not to go to the library tomorrow night.

무엇으로 서울에 가기로 했습니까?
By what (mode of transport) did you decide to go to Seoul?

The sentence ending -기는 하다

This ending is used to express a speaker's intention to acknowledge the message of the main verb, but to refer to another message by way of contrast. It is equivalent to the expression, "It's true, but . . ."

저는 서울을 좋아하기는 합니다.	It's true that I like Seoul, but . . .
금시계 값은 비싸기는 해요.	It's true that a golden watch is expensive, but . . .
그 여자는 미인이기는 합니다.	Everybody knows that she is a real beauty, but . . .

The sentence ending -(으)면 안 되다

This ending is used to express the prohibition of a certain act by a speaker. It is a negative counterpart of the Korean expressions "-어야 하다" or "-어도 좋다," and is equivalent to "should not," or "must not."

너무 늦게 가면 안 돼요.	You must not go too late.
공원 풀밭에 들어가면 안 됩니다.	You must not enter the grass area of the park.

The temporal conjunction -동안에

This conjunction is used to express the duration of an action or process. The English equivalent is "while doing something."

내가 여기에서 기다리는 동안에 무얼 하겠어요?	While I wait here, what are you going to do?
밥 먹는 동안에 전화가 두번 왔어요.	While (one) ate, two phone calls came.

Exercises

10 You have a lot of things to do piled up in the office. Suggest that your colleague finishes (up) doing three things for you this afternoon.

11 You have a date with a friend at Chongro. Someone in the office asks you when you are supposed to meet him. Tell him that you agreed to meet at 4 P.M.

12 The weather has been so unpredictable that you have had difficulty deciding how to travel. One day a friend asks you what you have decided on. Tell him that you have made up your mind to go by train.

13 You have been living in Seoul for a number of years. One day an American newcomer to your company asks you how you like living in Seoul. Tell him that you like living in Seoul, but you have some reservations.

14 Recently, a male college graduate joined the company. Everybody is envious of his intelligence and hard work, but to you he seems somewhat impolite. Someone in the office asks you whether you like him. Tell your colleague that he is a good worker, but not the type of person you like.

15 In the park children try to jump over a picket sign that reads "Keep off the grass." Tell them not to go in there.

16 Your younger brother watches TV for three hours a day. Tell him that he shouldn't watch TV for so long.

17 You are secretary to the company president. One day, when he was in a meeting, you received three phone calls for him. After his meeting, he asks you whether anybody called. Tell him that, during the meeting, three people called.

18 You are at the service station and your car has broken down. Tell the manager that your car needs a checkup.

19 At the repair shop, a mechanic asks you what kind of problem you are having with you car. Tell him that your heard a very strange noise while driving sometime ago.

20 Translate the following dialogue into Korean:

A: How can I help you, sir?
B: My car seems to have a problem.

A: What kind of problem is it?
B: The engine feels very hot.
A: Let me check. Ah, the coolant has all leaked out.

21 Complete the dialogue:

A. 차 고칠 수 있어요?
B.
A. 잘 모르겠는데요.
B.
A. 몇 시간 걸리죠?
B.
A. 안 되겠는데요.
　　두 시간 후에 친구하고 약속이 있거든요.

22 Reading passage 🔲 Sandra Hopkins has recently bought a new car, a Lemans made in Korea. She is very proud of it, so she and her friend go for a long drive. But while on their way, the car runs into a problem. Try to figure out how serious the problem is and how it affects their plans for the day.

쌘드라씨는 한국에서 생산되는 르망차를 최근에 샀다. 새 차를 처음 운전할 때는 가슴이 조마조마하기도 했다. 어느 여름 오후에 쌘드라씨는 직장 동료인 수진씨와 교외로 놀러 갔다. 차가 고속도로를 따라 달릴 때는 기분이 신났다. 고속도로에서 한 두 시간 달린 후였다. 그런데 갑자기 차에서 이상한 소리가 나기 시작했다. 둘은 겁이 나기도 하고, 걱정도 되어 차를 주유소로 몰고 갔다. 정비원 아저씨가 뚜껑을 열고 점검을 했다. 아저씨는 라지에타에서 물이 다 새어 나가 버렸다고 했다. 차를 고쳐서 집으로 그냥 돌아왔다. 재수가 없는 날이었다.

Key words

르망차	Lemans car	기분	(one's) mood
생산되다	be manufactured	신나다	get excited
조마조마하다	nervous	겁이 나다	is scared
직장 동료	colleague	걱정이 되다	is worried
교외	suburb	재수	luck

20 병원에서
At the hospital

By the end of this lesson you should be able to:
- talk about your illness
- use the sentence endings -ㄴ(은)적이 있다, -는지 물어보겠다, -아(어/여)있다, -(이)던가요?, -(이)라고 생각되다
- use the conjunctions -(으)면서, -아(어/여)도, -ㄹ(을)테니
- use the noun suffix -ㄹ(을) 정도로
- use the particle -도록
- use the idiomatic expressions 한 숨도 못 잤다; 아파죽겠다

Dialogue 1 🔲🔲 *Anthony Miller fell ill last night, so he couldn't get a wink of sleep. The next morning he rushed to the emergency room of a private hospital and asked whether he could be examined immediately*

간호사: 어디가 아프세요?
밀러: 저 머리가 아프고 온 몸이 쑤셔요.
간호사: 열은 어때요?
밀러: 열이 40도까지 올라간 적도 있어요.
　　　 열이 많아서 밤새도록 한 숨도 못 잤어요.
간호사: 그래요? 응급환자를 받을 수 있는지 물어 볼게요.
　　　 잠깐 기다리세요.
밀러: 예, 감사합니다.
간호사: 오늘은 감기 환자가 너무 밀려 있어요.
　　　 두시간 후에 다시 올 수 있어요?
밀러: 지금 너무 아파 죽겠어요.
간호사: 그럼, 이리 빨리 들어 오세요.

Vocabulary

아프다	hurt	응급환자	emergency patient
머리	head		

온 몸	all body parts	감기	cold
도(온도)	centigrade	밀려있다	backlogged
올라가다	go up	아파 죽겠다	dying of pain
밤새도록	until the end of the night	간호사	nurse
		밀러	Miller
한 숨	one wink of sleep	40도	40°C
		물어보다	ask
쑤시다	ache	열	fever

Language points

The sentence ending -(은) 적이 있다

This ending is used to express one's experience in the past. Its meaning is equivalent to the expression "one has done something." It is interchangeable with the sentence ending -ㄴ(은) 일이 있다.

일본에 가본 적이 있어요.
I have been to Japan.

전에 김선생님은 은행에서 돈을 빌린 적이 있다.
Mr. Kim has borrowed money from the bank.

멕시코 음식을 먹은 적이 있는데, 맛이 좋았어요.
I have had Mexican food, (and) it's delicious.

멕시코 음식을 먹은 일이 있는데, 맛이 아주 좋았어요.
I have had Mexican food, (and) it tasted fantastic.

The particle -도록

This ending is attached to the verb and indicates the continuation of the action of a verb to a specified limit. It is equivalent to the preposition "until."

오늘 아침에는 해가 뜨도록 잤어요. This morning I overslept until the sun rose.
밤이 새도록 책을 읽었어요. I read a book until (the) morning.

The sentence ending -는지 물어 보다

This ending is attached to the end of an interrogative clause within the main sentence. The same ending is used for past, present, and future tense. The English equivalent is "one asks when/if ..."

언제 김선생님이 사무실에 돌아 오는지 물어 봤어요.
I asked when Mr. Kim would return to his office.

언제 기차가 역에 도착했는지 물어 봤어요.
I asked when the train arrived at the station.

언제 그 사람이 여기에 오겠는지 물어 봤어요.
I asked when he would come here.

The sentence ending -아(어/여) 있다

This ending is attached to the stem of such intransitive verbs as "go," "come," "stand up," "sit down." It expresses the location of an object or the continuation of an action that has already taken place.

책이 책상 위에 놓여 있다.   There is a book on the desk.
거리에 차가 많이   A lot of cars are backed up on
밀려 있다.   the streets.

The noun suffix -ㄹ(을) 정도로

This suffix is attached to a noun and indicates an extent to which the verb of a first clause affects one. The English equivalent is "to the extent that ..."

죽을 정도로 머리가 아파요.
I suffered a headache that was (*lit.* to the extent that it was) almost killing me.

내 친구가 달리는 정도로 나도 잘 달릴 수 있어요.
I can run as fast as (*lit.* to the extent that I am as fast as) my friend.

Idiomatic expressions

한 숨도 못 잤다 fail to get even a wink of sleep; 아파 죽겠다 dying of pain

어제 저녁에 너무 더워서 한 숨도 못 잤어요.
I couldn't get even a wink of sleep due to the heat last night.

너무 오래 걸어서 다리가 아파 죽겠어요.
The pain caused by the long walk is killing me.

Exercises

1 You are in the emergency room of a Korean hospital, and a nurse asks how high your body temperature went up to that night. Tell her that it reached 41°C on occasions.

2 Someone tells you that he has finished Hemingway's novel *For Whom the Bell Tolls*. Tell him that you have read that novel also.

3 A colleague says that you look pale. Tell him that you didn't get a wink of sleep last night.

4 You receive a phone call for Section Chief Hwang, and you think he is wrapped up at work. Tell the caller that you will ask Hwang if he can get to the phone right now.

5 A friend of yours asks you to go climbing on Saturday. Tell him that you have too many things to do.

6 In the examination room of a hospital, a doctor asks you how severe the pains in your stomach are. Tell him that they are almost killing you.

7 Someone comments that your eyes are red and are bugging out a bit. Tell him the reason why you didn't get a wink of sleep all night.

8 Arrange the words of the dialogue to make sense:

a 올라간, 적이, 39도까지, 어제 밤에, 열이, 있어요.
b 물어, 응급환자를, 있는지, 볼게요, 받을 수
c 감기, 오늘은,. 밀려, 환자가, 많이, 있어요

9 Translate the following dialogue into Korean:

A. Which part of your body hurts the most?
B. I have a headache.

A. How severe is it?
B. It's so severe (that) I couldn't get a wink of sleep.
A. Oh, too bad. Let me examine you first.

10 Complete the dialogue:

A: 어디가 아프세요?
B:
A: 어떻게 목이 아파요?
B:
A: 맞아요. 목이 부었습니다.
B: ·
A. 감기 증상인 것 같아요.

Culture point

When foreign travelers get sick, they can get medical treatment at such general hospitals as the Severance Hospital or the Asian Medical Center, where doctors and nurses speak some English. An emergency visit may involve a couple of hours' waiting in a crowded waiting room. However, if you can manage some Korean conversation, you can, of course, get medical treatment for a minor illness from a privately owned local hospital. If some medical emergency should occur on the street or open area, you can ask a passerby for assistance, since it is unlikely that you will see a policeman patroling on the Korean streets. Or, you can call for an ambulance from Asia Emergency Assistance, which provides a 24-hour emergency service for foreigners. For colds and other minor ailments, you can purchase appropriate medicine at Korean drugstores, which are on virtually every street corner. It is legal for a Korean pharmacist to prescribe medicine on the basis of symptoms described by the patient.

Dialogue 2 ▭ *The doctor examines Mr. Miller and prescribes some medicine for him*

의사: Anthony Miller씨죠? 어디가 아프죠?
밀러: 고열이 나면서 두통이 심해요.
의사: 옷을 벗고 저기 진찰대 위에 누우세요.
밀러: (진찰대 위에 누우면서) 이렇게 말입니까?
의사: 예. 배를 이렇게 눌러도 안 아프지요?
밀러: 안 아파요.
의사: 목은 아프지 않던가요?
밀러: 예. 편도선이 부은 것 같아요.

의사: 걱정 마세요. 유행성 독감이라고 생각돼요.
밀러   감기약을 처방해 줄테니 잠깐 기다리세요.
간호원: (처방전을 주면서) 네 시간마다 한 봉지씩 드세요.
밀러: 예. 감사합니다.

Vocabulary

고열	high fever	편도선	tonsil
두통	headache	붓다	swell
심하다	severe	걱정 마세요	don't worry
옷	clothes	유행성독감	contagious flu
벗다	take off	생각되다	come to think
진찰대	examination table	감기약	cold medicine
눕다	lie down	처방해주다	give (someone) a
말	word		prescription
배	belly	처방전	prescription
누르다	press	네 시간마다	every four hours
목	neck	봉지	bag

Language points

The conjunction -(으)면서

This attaches to the stem of an action verb and expresses two actions in combination. It translates as "while doing..."

학생들이 점심을 먹으면서 책을 읽고 있습니다.
While having lunch, students read books.

John은 잠 자면서 코를 골아요.
John snores while sleeping.

The conjunction -아(어/여)도

This conjunction is attached to the stem of any verb and expresses the contrast in value between the first and second clauses. The English equivalent is "even if..."

오늘은 비가 와도 바닷가에 갈거예요.
I'll go to the beach even if it does rain.

Mary는 김치가 매워도 잘 먹어요.
Mary eats Kimchi well even if it is hot and spicy.

내 동생은 공부를 열심히 해도, 성적은 좋지 않아요.
My younger brother doesn't get good grades even if he studies hard.

The sentence ending -(이)던가요?

This is attached to the stem of any verb and asks an informal question. The suffix 이 is taken after the linking verb (see Lesson 6).

배가 아플 때 열이 나던가요?
Do you experience a hot fever when your stomach aches?

이과장님 지금 사무실에 계시던가요?
Do you know that Section Chief Lee is now in his office?

그분 직업이 회사원이던가요?
Do you know he is a man working for the company?

The sentence ending -(이)라고 생각되다

This sentence ending is attached to a noun and indicates what a speaker thinks about the included sentence. The sentence ending -고 하다 is used for all other sentences that end in -다, except the sentence that uses the linking verb.

저분은 국민학교 선생님이라고 생각돼요.
I think that that person is a teacher at an elementary school.

저 건물은 육삼빌딩이라고 생각돼요.
I think that the building over there is the 63 building.

미국 학생들은 한국어 공부를 열심히 한다고 생각돼요.
I think that American students study (the) Korean (language) very hard.

The causal conjunction - ㄹ(을)테니

In a two-clause sentence, this ending is attached to the stem of any action verb in the first clause and explains a reason or cause for the second clause (which can take an imperative, request, or interrogative form).

곧 나올테니, 여기서 기다리세요.
Since I will come out shortly, please wait here.

기차가 십분 후면 도착할테니, 플렛트 홈에서 기다립시다.
Since the train will arrive in ten minutes, let's wait on the platform.

Exercises

11 You are in the examination room of a hospital and a physician asks you how bad the symptoms of your cold are. Tell him that you have pains in your throat and you also have a severe headache.

12 Noticing that you look tired, a friend asks how you feel. Tell him that, although you didn't feel too good, you got to work today.

13 A doctor examines part of your stomach and asks you whether it hurts you. Tell him that, even if he presses hard, it doesn't hurt you too much.

14 A colleague tells you about a recent bout of flu. Ask him if his temperature went up to 40°C.

15 You are not sure whether Section Chief Lee is in his office right now, and you happen to notice that his secretary is nearby. Ask her if he is in his office.

16 You are taking a friend who has come to visit Seoul on a tour. Looking up at the tallest building in the vicinity, she asks you what building it is. Tell her that you think that it's the 63 building.

17 You are distributing some supplies to the people in your office, and they are swarming around you to get things first. Tell them that, since everybody will get supplies, they should stand in line.

18 Correct your friend's grammar:

a 배 누르면 아프지 안던가요?
b 감기약을 처방해 준 터이니, 여기서 기다리세요.
c 요즈음 유행하는 독감이다고 생각됩니다.

19 Translate the following dialogue into Korean:

A: Where does it really hurt you (i.e., hurt badly)?
B: I have a high temperature and my throat really hurts.

A: Can you get up on the examination table and lie down?
B: Do you mean like this?
A: Yeah. That's it.
B: When I press here, do you feel any pain?
A: I don't think I feel any pain there.

20 Complete the dialogue:

A. 어디가 아프시죠?
B.
A. 옷을 벗고 이 진찰대 위에 누우세요.
B.
A 예, 좋습니다. 배를 누르면 어디가 아픕니까?
B.
A. 목은 아프지 않던가요?
B.
A. 위가 나쁜 것 같습니다.

21 Reading passage ◖◗ Anthony Miller came down with a high fever yesterday, so he had to stay in bed all day. When he couldn't stand the pain anymore, he went to a hospital in the neighborhood. After the doctor examined him, he gave him a prescription. Anthony fell into a deep sleep only after taking some medication for his high fever. Try to figure out what kinds of symptoms he showed and how often he was told to take medication every day.

Anthony Miller씨는 어제 저녁부터 몸이 불편하여 침대에 누워 있었다. 열이 40도까지 올라간 적이 있고, 배도 아파서 잠을 잘 수가 없었다. 더 이상 참을 수가 없어서 11시경에 근처에 있는 개인병원의 응급실에 갔다. 응급실에는 감기 환자들이 많이 몰려 있어서 매우 혼잡했다. 한시간 정도 기다린 후에 의사 선생님의 진찰을 받을 수 있었다. 의사 선생님은 진찰을 한 후에 해열제 약을 지어 주면서 4시간마다 먹으라고 했다. Miller씨는 집에 돌아와 약을 먹고 잠을 잘 수 있었다.

Key words

불편하다	feel uncomfortable	몰리다	crowded with people
열	fever		
아프다	ache (verb)	진찰을 받다	be examined
참다	put up with	해열제	medication for high fever
개인병원	private hospital		
응급실	emergency room	지어주다	prescribe

Key to exercises

Introduction: Korean sounds and Hangul

Unit 1 Vowels

Exercise 1

1 우   2 오   3 에   4 애   5 어

Exercise 2

1 에   2 오   3 애   4 아   5 어

Exercise 3 (Individual practice)

Exercise 4 (Individual practice)

Unit 2 Nine consonants

Exercise 5 (Individual practice)

Exercise 6 (Individual practice)

Exercise 7

1 너   2 베   3 다   4 지   5 제주

Exercise 8

1 모조   2 강동   3 베드   4 조미   5 누저

Exercise 9

1 ㄴ 2 ㅓ 3 ㄹ 4 ㅁ 5 ㅅ

Unit 3 Diphthongs

Exercise 10

1 야 2 구 3 져 4 베 5 려
6 마 7 교 8 재 9 료 10 겨

Exercise 11

1 야구 2 교사 3 여유 4 여자 5 여우
6 요리 7 예사 8 조서 9 자유 10 애기

Exercise 12 (Individual practice)

Exercise 13 (Individual practice)

Exercise 14

1 뭬 2 쉬 3 과 4 뷔 5 쉐
6 뉘 7 봐 8 쥐 9 뤼 10 웨

Exercise 15

1 겨자 2 종이 3 선박 4 양력 5 벽지
6 술병 7 객석 8 달력 9 날개 10 양복

Exercise 16

1 ㅏ 2 ㅗ 3 ㅏ 4 ㅁ 5 ㅇ, ㅕ

Unit 4 Aspirated consonants

Exercise 17 (Individual practice)

Exercise 18 (Individual practice)

Exercise 19

1 총	2 벙	3 직	4 차리	5 타방
6 바리	7 차리	8 벌덕	9 헌대	10 추기

Exercise 20

1 람 몇   2 침 잿   3 명 팁   4 빛 맻   5 캥 거

Exercise 21

1 ㅊ   2 ㅅ   3 ㅎ   4 ㄱ   5 ㅐ

Exercise 22

1 퍼   2 토   3 차 칭

Unit 5 Double consonants

Exercise 23 (Individual practice)

Exercise 24 (Individual practice)

Exercise 25

1 거	2 꾸	3 도	4 똘	5 뿡
6 더	7 돌	8 검	9 깔	10 달

Exercise 26

1 까다	2 그다	3 꼬다	4 달랑	5 끙끙
6 조석	7 짤다	8 쩍쩍	9 푸다	10 쓰다

Exercise 27

1 까다	2 크다	3 꼬다	4 딸랑	5 쿵쿵
6 쫑	7 짤다	8 치다	9 꿀	10 푸다

Exercise 28

1 ㄲ   2 ㅉ   3 ㄸ   4 ㅃ   5 ㅆ

Unit 6 Summary, word structure, and other aspects of Korean

Korean alphabet bingo game

The letters called are: 가, 요, 토, 루, 차, 파, 마, 뚱, 깔, 꺼, 찌

Lesson 1

1 a 김선생님, 안녕하세요?   b 이교수님, 안녕하세요?
   c 박과장님, 안녕하세요?   d 미스 강, 안녕하세요?

2 a 김선생님, 안녕하십니까?   b 사장님, 안녕하십니까?
   c 장선생님, 안녕하십니까?

3 a 잘 지냅니다.   b 그저 그래요.
   c 요즈음 바쁘게 지냅니다.

4 a 예, 오래간만입니다.   b 미스 리, 안녕하세요?
   c 요즈음 어떻게 지내세요?   d 김교수님, 안녕하십니까?

5 a 강 기 수   b 박 상 달   c 김 근 영

6 a 미스터 김   b 미스 한
   c 미스 나   d 미스터 신

7 a 진선생님, 요즈음 어떻게 지내세요(어떠세요)?
   b 미스 황, 요즈음 어떻게 지내세요(어떠세요)?
   c 박과장님, 요즈음 어떻게 지내세요(어떠세요)?
   d 미스 리, 요즈음 어떻게 지내세요(어떠세요)?

8 a 교회에 가세요?   b 도서관에 가세요?
   c 식당에 가세요?   d 우체국에 가세요?

9 a 교회에 안 가요?   b 도서관에 안 가요?
   c 집에 안 가요?   d 우체국에 안 가요?

10 a 강선생님은 별로 안 바쁘세요.
  b 미스터 리는 별로 안 좋으세요.
  c 미스 진은 교회에 안 가세요.
  d 최교수님은 도서관에 별로 안 가세요.

Lesson 2

1 저 *your name* 입니다. (e.g.: 저 강영수 입니다.)

2 a 이분이 메리 진입니다.   b 이분이 김교수님입니다.
  c 이분이 메리 스미쓰입니다.

3 a 우리가   b 내 친구가   c 책상이

4 a 교회에 가겠어요.   b 공부하겠어요.
  c 도서관에 가겠어요.

5 a D   b I   c R   d R

6 아니오, 모릅니다.

7 이분 알아요.

8 안녕히 계세요.

9 네, 안녕히 가십시오.

10 a 이분이 미스터 김입니다.   b 이분이 박과장님입니다.
  c 이분이 미스 황입니다.

11 a 우리   b 그 사람   c 저희

12 a 처음 뵙겠습니다.   b 인사하세요.
  c 이분이 제니 리씨입니다.   d 가 봐야겠습니다.
  e 다음에 또 뵙겠습니다.

Lesson 3

1 a 집에 계세요.   b 커피 드세요.
  c 바쁘세요.

2 a 집에 계십니다.   b 커피 드십니다.
  c 바쁘십니다.

3 a 우유 드시겠어요?　　b 맥주 드시겠어요?
c 인삼차 드시겠어요?　　d 사이다 드시겠어요?

4 a 이리 앉으세요. / 이리 앉으십시오.
b 이리 오세요. / 이리 오십시오.
c 들어가세요. / 들어가십시오.

5 a 김선생님이 여기 앉으세요.　　b 이선생님 주무세요.
c 장박사님이 지금 집에 가세요.

6 a 김선생님이 여기 앉으십니다.　　b 이선생님 주무십니다.
c 장박사님이 지금 집에 가십니다.

7 A: 수고하십니다. 미스 장 계세요?
B: 네, 계세요. 누구세요?
A: 사업친구입니다
B: 잠깐 기다리세요.
A: 네, 감사합니다.

8 a 눈이 와서 교회에 안 가요.　　b 바빠서 교회에 안 가요.
c 너무 피곤해서 교회에 안 가요.

9 a 미스 진의 책이에요.　　b 켈리교수님의 책이에요.
c 박선생님의 책이에요.

10 a 오늘은 피곤해서 공부 안 해요.
b 요즈음 장사가 잘 돼요.
c 오늘은 내 친구를 만나서 기분이 매우 좋아요.
d 이선생님은 요즈음 매우 바빠요.

11 a 덕택에 잘 지냅니다.　　b 지금 바빠서, 집에 못 가요.
c 이선생님의 책이에요.

Lesson 4

1 a 롯데호텔에 어떻게 갑니까?　　b 지하철역에 어떻게 갑니까?
c 종로에 어떻게 갑니까?

2 a 여기가 시청입니까?　　b 여기가 국회의사당입니까?
c 여기가 우체국입니까?　　d 여기가 동대문시장입니까?

3 a 거기가 미국 대사관입니다.　　b 저기가 신라호텔입니다.
　 c 여기가 백화점입니다.　　　　d 거기가 은행입니다.
　 e 여기가 경찰서입니다.

4 시청, 역, 우체국

5 a 저쪽으로 어떻게 건너갑니까?
　 b 오른쪽으로 돌아 지하도로 건너가세요.
　 c 여기가 대사관이 아닙니다.

6 a 거기가 지하철역입니다.
　 b 여기는 서울이 아닙니다.
　 c 거기가 시청이 아닙니다.
　 d 이선생님은 지금 안 바쁘세요.

7 A: 실례합니다. 이 근처에 경찰서가
　　　 어디 있습니까?
　 B: 바로 길 건너편에 있습니다.
　 A: 이 거리를 어떻게 건너갑니까? 거기는 교통이 혼잡합니다.
　 B: 글쎄요, 모퉁이에 있는 지하도를 이용하세요.
　 A: 알겠습니다. 대단히 감사합니다.
　 B: 천만에요.

8 Model answer
　 MR. ANDERSON:　실례합니다. 여기가 플라자 호텔입니까?
　 STUDENT:　　　아니오. 저기가 플라자 호텔입니다.
　 MR. ANDERSON:　저쪽으로 어떻게 갑니까?
　 STUDENT:　　　왼쪽으로 곧장 가세요.
　 MR. ANDERSON:　예, 감사합니다.
　 STUDENT:　　　천만에요. 조심해서 가세요.

9 a 신문 읽어요.　　　　b 테니스 해요.
　 c 영화 봐요(보아요).　　d 정원 손질해요.

10 a 시간이 있으면 이탈리아로 여행을 가겠어요.
　　 b 백만 달러가 있으면 이탈리아로 여행을 가겠어요.
　　 c 비행기가 있으면 이탈리아로 여행을 가겠어요.

11 (Individual answer)

12 a 배로 서울에 갑니다.　　b 비행기로 서울에 갑니다.
　　 c 기차로 서울에 갑니다.

13 a 버스 정류장에 어떻게 갑니까?   b 은행에 어떻게 갑니까?
   c 도서관에 어떻게 갑니까?

14 a 서울에 기차로 가면 오래 걸려요.
   b 오른쪽으로 가면 극장이 보여요.
   c 모퉁이를 지나가면 우체국이 있어요.

15 a 택시로 가세요.   b 버스로 가세요.
   c 지하철로 가세요.   d 리무진으로 가세요.

16 a 고속버스에서 내리면, 바로 정면에 큰 건물이 보일거예요.
   b 그 건물 왼쪽으로 지나면, 다른 작은 건물이 보일거예요.
   그것이 박물관이에요.
   c 매표소에서 표를 사세요.
   d 중심로를 따라서 곧장 후문으로 가세요. 거기 제가 있을거예요.

17 Model answer
   이 길을 지나 사거리까지 ("up to the intersection") 가세요.
   거기서 왼쪽으로 곧장 가세요.

Lesson 5

1 a 호텔   b 집
   c 도서관   d 집

2 a 서울에 갑니다.   b 고향에 갑니다.
   c 뉴욕에 갑니다.   d 보스턴에 갑니다.

3 a 기차로 갑니다.   b 고속버스로 갑니다.
   c 차로 갑니다.   d 택시로 갑니다.

4 a 여기가 시청입니다. (지도를 보면서)
   b 여기가 지하철역입니다. (지도를 보면서)
   c 여기가 미국 대사관입니다. (지도를 보면서)

5 A: 김선생님 어디 가세요?
   B: 지하철역에 갑니다.
   A: 누가 옵니까?
   B: 네, 내 동생이 와요. 내일이 내 아들 생일이에요.
   A: 그래요? 좋으시겠어요.

6 a 누가 서울역에 옵니까?　　b 서울역이 저기에 있습니까?
　c 뉴욕에 기차로 가요.　　　d 주말에 친구 집에 가요.
　e 친구가 집에 가요.

7 Model answer
　YOU:　　　　어디 가세요?
　COLLEAGUE: 영국 대사관에 갑니다.
　YOU:　　　　대사관이 어디 있습니까?
　COLLEAGUE: 저기가 바로 대사관입니다.
　YOU:　　　　그럼, 다녀 오세요.
　COLLEAGUE: 예, 안녕히 가세요.

8 a 교회 가요.　　b 집 가요.
　c 역 가요.　　　d 도서관 가요.

9 a 아침에 도서관에 가요.　　b 오후에 도서관에 가요.
　c 정오에 도서관에 가요.　　d 저녁에 도서관에 가요.

10 a 형님께서 오세요.　　　b 아버님께서 오세요.
　c 어머님께서 오세요.　　d 삼촌께서 오세요.

11 a 눈이 많이 왔거든요.　　b 늦잠 잤거든요.
　c 친구가 왔거든요.　　　d 집에 갔거든요.

12 a 뉴욕에서 왔어요.　　　b 요하네스버그에서 왔어요.
　c 시드니에서 왔어요.　　d 고향에서 왔어요.

13 a 내일 형님이 한국에서 오세요.
　b 제 생일이 월말이거든요.
　c 지금 어머님께서 지하철역 가세요.
　d 지금 비가 많이 오거든요.

14 a 주말에 친구 집에 가요.　　　　b 아버지께서 교회에 가세요.
　c 친구가 식당에서 점심 먹어요.　　d 편지가 서울에서 왔어요.

15 line 1. — 주무세요　　　line 2. — 자요?
　line 3. — 주무세요　　　line 4. — 잡니다
　line 5. — 주무십니까?

16 아버지께서 고향에서 오십니다.

Lesson 6

1 a 그것은 의자입니다.　　b 그것은 신문입니다.
　 c 그것은 사전입니다.　　d 그것은 지도입니다.

2 a 아니오, 그것은 의자입니다.
　 b 아니오, 저것은 오늘 신문이 아닙니다.
　 c 예, 그것은 메모지입니다.
　 d 예, 그것은 연필입니다.

3 a 아니오, 저분은 간호사입니다.
　 b 아니오, 이분은 누나가 아닙니다.
　 c 아니오, 이분은 남자가 아닙니다.

4 a 그것은 연필이에요.　　b 그것은 펜이에요.
　 c 그것은 책이에요.　　d 그것은 지도이에요.

5 a 자는 있어요.　　b 한국지도는 있어요.
　 c 클립은 있어요.　　d 공책은 있어요..

6 a 아니오, (연필) 없어요.　　b 예, (시계) 있어요.
　 c 예, (열쇠) 있어요.

7 a 미스 리는 식당에 있습니다.
　 b 톰슨 과장님은 휴게실에 계십니다.
　 c 비서 미스 홍은 간이식당에 있습니다.

8 a 스카치 테이프는 없는데요.　　b 스테플러는 없는데요.
　 c 가위는 없는데요.

9 a 볼펜 좀 갖다 주겠어요?　　b 메모지 좀 갖다 주겠어요?
　 c 클립 좀 갖다 주겠어요?　　d 잉크 좀 갖다 주겠어요?

10 (Individual answers)

Lesson 7

1 a 신문 봤습니다(봤어요).　　b 영화관에 갔습니다(갔어요).
　 c 한국어 공부했습니다(했어요).

2 a 점심 밖에서 하실까요(하시겠어요)?
　 b 차 한잔 하실까요(하시겠어요)?
　 c 슈퍼마켓에 가실까요(가시겠어요)?

3 a 점심 밖에서 합시다. b 차 한잔 합시다.
c 슈퍼마켓에 갑시다.

4 a 데이트 했어요? b 텔레비전 봤어요?
c 여행했어요?

5 a 구내식당이 어떻겠습니까? b 신라식당이 어떻겠습니까?
c 다미정이 어떻겠습니까?

6 신라식당은 깨끗하고 값이 싸요.

7 a 구내 식당이 어떻겠습니까?
b 간이 식당이 어떻겠습니까?
c Korea House (한국의 집) 식당이 어떻겠습니까?

8 A: 점심(식사)하셨어요?
B: 아니오, 아직 안했습니다.
A: 점심 식사하러 같이 나가실까요?
B: 네, 그러십시다.
A: 구내 식당이 어떻겠습니까?
B: 네, 그곳은 크고 값이 매우 싸요.

9 여기 비빔밥 하나 주세요.

10 저도 불고기 백반을 시키지요.

11 a 비빔 냉면 주세요. b 냉면 둘 주세요.
c 세 명입니다.

12 비빔밥 하나, 갈비탕 하나 주세요.

13 이번에는 제가 내겠습니다.

14 Model answer:
a 아니요. 아직 하지 않았어요.
b 집에서 하겠어요.
c 냉면을 시키겠어요.

15 A: 어서 오세요. 몇 분이세요?
B: 두 명입니다.
A: 뭘 주문하시겠어요?

B: 불고기 백반 하나, 만두국 하나 주세요.
A: 조금만 기다리세요.

16 a 철희씨는 오늘 회사에 출근하지 않았다.
 b 불고기 둘 주세요.
 c 식사 많이 드세요.
 d Goldsmith씨도 김밥을 시켰어요.

17 영자씨, 저녁식사 같이 하시겠어요?

18 a 불고기 백반 주세요. b 불고기 정식 주세요.
 c 만두국 주세요.

19 Goldsmith씨는 비빔냉면이 너무 매워서 다 먹지 못했다.

Lesson 8

1 a 보다 (action verb) b 이다 (linking verb)
 c 있다 (existential verb) d 많다 (adjectival verb)

2 그 영화는 좋았는데, 너무 길었어요.

3 음식은 좋았지만, 값이 너무 비쌌어요.

4 a 책 읽었어요. b 텔레비젼 영화 봤어요.
 c 아무 것도 안했어요.

5 a 열심히 공부했지만 잘 이해가 되지 않았어요.
 b 많이 먹지만 살이 찌지 않아요.
 c 이 상품은 값이 싸지만 품질이 좋아요.

6 a 좋은 b 큰 c 비싼

7 Model answer:
 a 영화관에 가요.
 b 아니요.
 c 예, 미스김하고 있어요.

8 a 미스 장 내일 저녁에 시간 있어요?
 b 미스 장 오늘 밤에 시간 있어요?
 c 미스 장 점심 때에 시간 있어요?

9 오늘은 안 되겠어요.

10 a 11시 25분입니다.   b 5시 반입니다.
   c 11시 10분 전입니다.

11 a 시험이 끝난 후에 극장에 갑시다.
   b 일이 끝난 후에 극장에 갑시다.

12 a 명동에 있는 식당에서 만나요.
   b 종로에 있는 식당에서 만나요.
   c 광화문에 있는 식당에서 만나요.

13 a 오후 세 시에 전화하세요.
   b 네 시 십오 분에 전화하세요.
   c 오전 아홉 시 십 분에 전화하세요.

14 a 아침 열 시에 제 남동생하고 약속이 있어요.
   b 정오에 제 어머니하고 점심 약속이 있어요.
   c 저녁에 이웃집 친구들하고 약속이 있어요.

15 (Individual answers)

16 A: 어제 저녁에 뭘 하셨어요?
   B: 제 친구들하고 극장에 갔어요.
   A: 영화 재미있었어요?
   B: 물론 재미있었지만, 너무 짧았어요.

17 많은 선수들이 다쳐서 두 사람은 기분이 별로 안 좋았다.

Lesson 9

1 a 용산 지하철역까지 갑니다.   b 미국 대사관까지 갑니다.
   c 김포 공항까지 갑니다.

2 동대문까지 얼마나 걸립니까?

3 a 종각까지 10분 걸립니다.
   b 동대문 운동장까지 30분 걸립니다.
   c 미국 대사관까지 50분 정도 걸립니다.

4 a 기차로 다섯시간 걸립니다.
   b 비행기로 한시간 걸립니다.
   c 고속버스로 네시간 반 걸립니다.

5 a 이것은 펜이고 저것은 연필입니다.
  b 이것은 컴퓨터이고 저것은 칠판입니다.
  c 이것은 책상이고 저것은 의자입니다.

6 a 왼쪽에 있는 건물은 무슨 건물이에요?
  b 오른쪽에 있는 건물은 무슨 건물이에요?
  c 저기 큰 건물은 무슨 건물이에요?

7 A: 어디까지 가십니까?
  B: 광화문에 있는 미국 대사관까지 갑니다.
  A: 어떤 길로 갈까요?
  B: 시청까지 가서 거기서 우회전 하세요.
  A: 알겠습니다.

8 a 제과점 앞에서 내려 줄 수 있어요?
  b 은행 앞에서 내려 줄 수 있어요?
  c 교회 앞에서 내려 줄 수 있어요?

9 요금이 얼마입니까?

10 a 도서관에 가서 신문을 읽겠습니다.
  b 술집에 가서 사람을 만나겠습니다.

11 a 장보러 갈 수 있어요. b 은행에 갈 수 있어요.
  c 방을 청소할 수 있어요.

12 만 사천원밖에 없어요.

13 a 책값이 얼마입니까? b 공책값이 얼마입니까?
  c 메모지값이 얼마입니까?

14 a 모자는 사천원에 샀습니다.
  b 옷은 사만 오천원에 샀습니다.

15 Model answer:
  a 교보빌딩 앞에서 내려 주세요.
  b 시청까지 갑니다.
  c 아니요, 저기 신호등 지나서 내려 주세요.

16 택시로 가시죠?

17 A: 여기서 내려 드릴까요?
B: 아니오, 앞으로 좀 더 가시겠어요?
A: 저기에는 설 수 없어요.
B: 그럼 저 네거리 지나서 내려줄 수 있어요?
A: 그렇게 하지요.
B: 택시 요금이 얼마입니까?
A: 육천 칠백원입니다.

18 운전기사 아저씨가 길을 잘 못 들어 시간이 더 많이 걸렸다. 그래서 택시비도 두배 지불해야했다.

Lesson 10

1 a 수건 사지 않겠어요.   b 청바지 사지 않겠어요.
c 반바지 사지 않겠어요.

2 a 사과가 배만큼 큽니다.   b 연필이 펜만큼 큽니다.

3 a ②번이 더 길어요.   b ②번이 더 커요.
c ②번이 더 돈이 많아요.

4 a ③번이 가장 뚱뚱해요.   b ①번이 가장 길어요.
c ②번이 가장 길어요.

5 a 넥타이가 비싼 것 같아요. b 신발이 비싼 것 같아요.
c 티셔츠가 비싼 것 같아요.

6 미도파 백화점이 괜찮아요.

7 A: 오늘 오후에 쇼핑 같이 가겠어요?
B: 오늘 오후에는 좀 바쁜데요.
A: 그럼, 내일은 어때요?
B: 내일은 시간이 있어요.
A: 내일 일이 끝난 후에 연락해요.

8 a 노란 가방은 얼마예요?   b 빨간 가방은 얼마예요?
c 파란 가방은 얼마예요?

9 a 파란 티셔츠 좀 볼 수 있어요?
b 빨간 티셔츠 좀 볼 수 있어요?
c 노란 티셔츠 좀 볼 수 있어요?

10 좀 깎을 수 없어요?

11 이 가방은 좋으나 사지 않겠어요.

12 a 이 지갑은 값이 비싼데요.
   b 이 양말은 값이 비싼데요.
   c 이 빨간 모자는 값이 비싼데요.

13 파란 가방만 주세요.

14 이 모자는 현금으로 지불할게요.

15 a John은 요즈음 도서관에서 공부 안 한다.
   b 저기 있는 반바지 주세요.
   c 빨간 바지 사겠어요.
   d 저 푸른 가방은 어때요?

16 A: 책가방 좀 볼 수 있어요?
   B: 보세요. 어떤 색을 좋아하세요?
   A: 하얀 색으로 주세요.
   B: 이것들은 하얀 가방이에요. 예쁘고 튼튼해 보여요.
   A: 이 밤색 가방은 얼마예요?
   B: 학생은 돈이 없으니까 많이 깎아서 사만 오천원이에요.
   A: 대단히 감사합니다.

17 Model answer:
   a 롯데 백화점에 갑니다.
   b 하얀색 양말을 신고 있어요.
   c 푸른색입니다.

18 민수는 물건값이 비싸서 빨간 시계를 살 수 없었다.

Lesson 11

1 a 서울시내 구경을 갈까합니다.
   b 비행기로 제주도에 갈까합니다.
   c 수영하러 갈까합니다.

2 삼십 오번이나 오십 육번 버스가 이태원에 갑니다.

3 a 이나 b 이나 c 나

4 a 이십 삼번하고 사십 오번이 시청에 갑니다.
  b 사십 육번하고 육십 칠번이 미국 대사관에 갑니다.

5 a 오전 열 시 삼십 분에 새마을호가 부산에 갑니다.
  b 오후 세 시 삼십 오 분에 무궁화호가 부산에 갑니다.

6 미도파 백화점에 갔다 왔어요.

7 A: 이번 주말에 뭘 하세요?
  B: 글쎄요. 비행기로 제주도에 갈까 합니다.
  A: 거기에서 누구 만나세요?
  B: 예, 제 삼촌이 거기 살아요.
  A: 아 그래요. 그럼 잘 다녀오세요.
  B: 그럴게요.

8 B: 미도파 백화점에 갔다 옵니다.
  B: 예쁜 티셔츠를 샀어요.
  B: 값이 쌌어요.
  B: 그렇게 하세요.

9 a 부산행 표 한 장 주세요. b 경주행 표 두 장 주세요.
  c 광주행 표 세 장 주세요.

10 설악산 가는 기차표를 어디서 팔아요?

11 부산행 표 한 장 주세요.

12 지금 육 번 홈에 들어 오고 있는 열차는 부산행입니까?

13 a 오늘 신문 읽고 있어요. b 친구들과 얘기하고 있어요.
  c 아무것도 안 하고 있어요.

14 지금 칠 번 홈에 있는 열차를 타세요.

15 a 지금 들어온 기차가 부산에 갑니다.
  b 도서관에서 잡지를 읽는 학생들은 공부를 잘한다.
  c 기차를 타는 손님들은 미국 사람들이다.

16 a 미국에 가는 비행기는 10시에 있어요.
   b 부산가는 고속버스 몇 시에 있어요?
   c 수원행 지하철 세 시에 있어요.

17 B: 부산까지 갑니다.
   B: 서울역에서 탔어요.
   B: 오후 4시에 도착합니다.

18 A: 이번 주말에 무엇하세요?
   B: 아마 뉴욕시에 갈 거예요.
   A: 뉴욕시에 어떻게 가세요?
   B: 차로 갈 거예요.
   A: 갔다가 언제 오세요?
   B: 일요일 저녁에 늦게 돌아올까 해요.

19 서울역에서 광주까지 네 시간이 걸렸다. 광주역에서
7번 버스를 타고 송정리에 있는 형님집으로갔다.

Lesson 12

1 a 양말을 여동생에게 주려고 샀습니다.
   b 볼펜을 삼촌께 드리려고 샀습니다.
   c 티셔츠를 할머니께 드리려고 샀습니다.

2 사전하고 펜을 샀습니다.

3 아프니까 회의에 참석 못했어요.

4 책이 재미 없으니까 보지 않았어요.

5 영화가 재미 없으니까 도중에 나왔어요.

6 아기가 방에서 자고 있으니까 조용히 하세요.

7 (Individual answers)

8 a 오월 육일입니다.　 b 오월 십오일입니다.
   c 목요일입니다.

9 예금 구좌를 개설하려고 왔어요.

10 A: 어떻게 오셨어요?
B: 예금 구좌를 개설하려고 왔어요.
A: 저기 표를 기입하세요.
B: 알았습니다.

11 B: 보통예금으로 하겠어요.
A: 그럼, 이 표에 서명하세요.
A: 저기서 잠깐 기다리세요.

12 a 김선생님은 현금을 찾으러 은행에 갔어요.
b 이과장님은 쉬러 휴게실에 갔어요.
c 홍비서는 봉급을 찾으러 입금 창구에 갔어요.

13 지갑을 찾으려면 계산대로 가세요.

14 예금 청구서에다가 비밀번호를 적고 서명하세요.

15 만원 짜리 다섯 장하고, 오천원 짜리 세 장으로 주세요.

16 a 도장이 필요해요.   b 여권이 필요해요.
c 비밀번호가 필요해요.

17 a 예금을 찾으려면 도장이 필요해요.
b 이름칸에 비밀번호도 쓰시고 도장을 찍으세요.
c 만원짜리 다섯장 필요해요.

18 A: 어떻게 오셨어요?
B: 예금하러 왔는데요.
A: 저기 있는 표를 기입하세요.
B: 알았습니다.

19 B: 예금을 찾으러 왔어요.
B: 오만원 찾겠습니다.
B: 여기 다 썼습니다.
B: 예, 알겠습니다.

20 예금을 찾으려면 여권이 필요해 호텔방에 가서 여권
을 가져왔지만 은행문이 닫혀서 현금을 찾을 수 없었다.

Lesson 13

1 늦어서 미안합니다.

2 교통이 막혀서 빨리 올 수 없어요.

3 방금 전(or 얼마전)에 김선생은 사무실에 있었어요.

4 비가 오기 전에 안으로 들어 갑시다.

5 a 지금 비가 오니까 안으로 들어 갑시다.
 b 바람이 부니까 건물 안으로 들어 가세요.
 c 학생들이 교실에 많이 있다.
 d 이사장님은 많은 돈이 있다.

6 a 언제나 서울역 앞은 교통이 밀려서 혼잡하다.
 b 시내에서 학생들이 데모해서 교통이 복잡하다.
 c 서울에서 많은 한국음식을 먹었었다.

7 A: 늦어서 미안해요.
 B: 괜찮아요.
 A: 버스를 탔는데, 교통이 막혀서 빨리 올 수 없었어요.
 B: 안됐어요. 대학생들이 데모했어요?
 A: 아니오. 교통사고가 시청 앞에서 났었어요.

8 B: 시청에 갔었어요.
 B: 예, 교통이 많이 막혔어요.
 B: 아니오. 학생들이 데모를 했었어요.

9 커피 한 잔 갖다 주세요.

10 책을 다 읽은 후에 갖다 드리지요.

11 잘 지냅니다.

12 읽을 책이 많아요.

13 a 동생한테(에게) 연필 줬어요.
 b 삼촌한테(에게) 자 드렸어요.
 c 언니한테(에게) 공책 줬어요.

14 a 일주일에 세시간씩 영회를 가르쳐요.
 b 일주일에 두시간씩 제민이를 가르쳐요.

15 그 일은 아주 힘들겠군요!

16 a 쉬어야해요.   b 책을 읽어야해요.
 c 제 동생하고 영화 보러 가야해요.

17 A: 요즈음 어떻게 지내세요?
   B: 바쁘게 지냅니다.
   A: 무슨 일이 그렇게 많아요?
   B: 요즈음 회의가 많이 있거든요.
   A: 아, 그래요? 매우 힘들겠군요.

18 B: 예 좀 바빴어요.
   B: 개인지도를 하고 있어요.
   B: 일주일에 6시간씩 가르치고 있어요.

19 주말여행에 관하여 이야기했고 버스를 타고 집으로 돌아
오는 길에 교통이 막혀서 택시를 타고 집으로 돌아왔다.

Lesson 14

1 방을 예약하지 못 했어요.

2 책을 다 못 읽었어요.

3 아직 쉬지 못했어요.

4 너무 바빠서 그 영화를 보지 못했어요.

5 주머니에 삼만원밖에 없어요.

6 저 스웨터 입어 볼 수 있어요?

7 아직 못 가봤어요.

8 온돌방에서 못 자는데요.

9 길 건너 다른 곳으로 가 봅시다.

10 A: 침대방 두 개 있어요?
   B: 여기는 침대방이 없으니까, 다른 여관으로 가보세요.
   A: 그럼 온돌방은 있어요?
   B: 예, 온돌방은 세 개 있습니다.

11 A: 몇 분이세요?
   B: 세 사람입니다.
   A: 온돌방 쓰시겠어요?

B: 아닙니다. 저희들은 외국인이니까 침대방을 쓰겠어요.
A: 침대방은 없는데요.
B: 아, 그래요. 옆에 있는 호텔로 가겠어요.

12 언제 회의가 있을지 몰라요.

13 a 새 옷을 사고 싶어요.
   b 제 여자친구 생일선물을 사고 싶어요.
   c 책을 세 권 사고 싶어요.

14 제 방은 몇 호실입니까?

15 그의 방은 몇 호실입니까?

16 5인용 침대방 있어요?

17 침대방 두 개하고 온돌방 하나가 필요해요.

18 A: 이 호텔에 침대방 있어요?
    B: 아니요. 이 호텔에는 온돌방만 있어요.
    A: 온돌방 하나에 얼마예요?
    B: 3만원인데요.

19 B: 예, 있어요.
    B: 방 하나에 4만원인데요.
    B: 예, 없어요.
    B: 그렇게 하지요.

20 여권을 가지고 가지 않아서 동료직원 헨리에게 전화를
    했다. 그가 여권 번호를 알려 주어서 투숙할 수 있었다.

Lesson 15

1 a Jane Kim이 나오기를 기다려요.
   b Thomas Moon이 나오기를 기다려요.
   c 이선생님이 나오기를 기다려요.

2 a 한국소설을 읽기 시작했어요.
   b 한국어를 공부하기 시작했어요.
   c 여자친구와 데이트하기 시작했어요.

3 4월에도 눈이 오는 때가 있어요.

4 123번 버스가 저기에 오네요!

5 직원들이 많이 불참했네요!

6 a 그는 여름이 오기를 기다린다.
　 b 갑자기 비가 오기 시작했다.
　 c Jane은 때로는 술을 많이 마시는 때가 있다.

7 A: 여름에도 눈이 오는 지역이 있다.
　 B: 사람들이 가을이 오기를 기다려요.
　 C: 한국의 기후는 사계절이 분명하다.

8 A: 한국의 여름 날씨는 어때요?
　 B: 대체로 더워요.
　 A: 비가 많이 와요?
　 B: 예, 여름은 장마철이라서 비가 많이 옵니다.

9 B: 대체로 시원해요.
　 B: 산에 등산 가요.
　 B: 아니오, 없어요.

10 a 책을 사러 가요.　　b 친구 만나러 가요.
　　 c 친구들과 놀러 가요.

11 a 미국에 돌아간 것 같아요.
　　 b 그의 여자 친구와 헤어진 것 같아요.
　　 c 사업차 여행한 것 같아요.
　　 d 아픈 것 같아요.

12 미국에서 온 어떤 학생이 공부하고 있는 것 같아요.

13 전보다 훨씬 젊어졌어요.

14 여름이 되면 날이 길어져요.

15 A: 한국의 가을 날씨는 어때요?
　　 B: 대체로 맑아요.
　　 A: 가을에 눈이 오는 때도 있어요?
　　 B: 아니오, 12월부터 눈이 오기 시작해요.
　　 A: 사람들은 가을에 무엇해요?
　　 B: 등산하러 산에 가요.

16 A: 오늘은 날씨가 아주 좋군요.
   A: 내일 뭐 하겠어요?
   A: 그럼, 혼자 갈거예요.

17 봄에는 산과 들에 꽃이 만발해서 아름다워요.
   여름에는 덥고 비가 많이 와서 별로 좋지 않아요.
   가을은 시원하고 겨울은 아주 춥고 눈도 많이 내려요.

Lesson 16

1 2년 전부터 한국어를 배우기 시작했어요.

2 10년 전부터 수영을 배웠어요.

3 a 동우가 미국으로 돌아갔다고 해요.
  b 동우가 아팠다고 해요.
  c 동우가 사라졌다고 해요.

4 회사가 가까워서 걸어 다녀요.

5 a 그는 사과를 좋아한다.
  b 그사람은 사과를 좋아한다.
  c John은 한국을 좋아해서 한국여자와 결혼했다.
  d 그 여학생은 내가 좋아하는 학생이에요.

6 a 회사 가까운 아파트에서 살아요.
  b 외국인 숙소에서 살아요.
  c 친척집에서 살아요.

7 불고기를 가장 좋아해요.

8 A: 지금 어디에서 사세요?
  B: 호암 숙소에서 살아요.
  A: 그 숙소는 회사에서 가까워요?
  B: 아니오, 아주 멀어요. 그래서, 매일 아침 버스 타고 다녀요

9 B: 외국인 숙소에서 살아요.
  B: 한달에 80만원이에요.
  B: 대체로 괜찮아요.
  B: 갈비를 가장 좋아해요.

10 남동생한테서 편지가 왔어요.

11 집에서 편지가 왔어요.

12 a belt는 한국어로 뭐라고 해요?
b purse는 한국어로 뭐라고 해요?
c pocket-size notebook은 한국어로 뭐라고 해요?

13 Model answer:
a 아니요. 교회에 가지 않았어요.
b 예, 안 갔어요.
c 예, 보겠어요.
d 아니요, 안 먹어 봤어요.

14 전화를 건 사람이 누구지요?

15 그 음식 참 맛있었어요.

16 공책에다가 받아 쓰세요.

17 전화 잘못 걸어서 미안합니다.

18 전화 잘못 거셨습니다.

19 A: 저한테 전화온 것 없었어요?
B: 예, KBS의 어떤 사람한테서 전화왔어요.
A: 그의 전화번호 있어요?
B: 여기 있어요.
A: 그에게 즉시 전화를 해 봐야겠어요.
B: 벌써 7시예요. 그는 아마 퇴근했을거예요.
A: 그렇군요. 내일 아침 전화하겠어요.

20 B:아니오, 안 계십니다.
B:아니오, 전화 잘못 거셨습니다.

21 택시 운전사는 Kerry씨의 영어 발음을 잘못 알아 듣고 Intercontinental Hotel에 내려주었다. 거기에 있는 경비원 아저
씨의 도움으로 택시를 타고 외국인 숙소로 갈 수 있었다.

Lesson 17

1 a 더 부유해지면 좋겠어요.　　b 승진하면 좋겠어요.
c 세계일주 여행을 하면 좋겠어요.

2 a 택시 잡기가 쉽지 않아요.
  b 잠을 잘 자기가 쉽지 않아요.
  c 미국음식을 찾기가 쉽지 않아요.

3 예, 파티에 가겠습니다. 감사합니다.

4 약도가 있으면 좋겠어요.

5 찾아갈 수 있을 것 같아요.

6 a 저기에 빨간 건물이 보여요.
  b 저기 있는 큰 건물을 봐요.
  c 큰 건물이 보이는 쪽에서 우리집은 왼쪽에 있습니다.

7 A: 이번 주말에 뭐 하세요?
  B: 한가해요.
  A: 저의 집에 오실 수 있어요?
  B: 그날이 무슨 날이에요?
  A: 아뇨, 시간을 함께 보내고 싶어서요.

8 B: 글쎄요.
  B: 오늘 저녁은 안되겠는데요, 선약이 있어요.
  B: 괜찮습니다.
  B: 예, 그렇게 합시다.

9 별거 아닙니다.

10 조금 늦어도 됩니다.

11 차린 음식들이 너무 맛있어 보입니다.

12 내일 만날때 책을 돌려주겠어요.

13 한국음식을 잘 먹는 편이에요.

14 A: 사장님은 출근했지만 회의에 참석하지 않았다.
   B: 차린 음식이 맛있어 보인다.
   A: 김치가 맵지만 저는 잘 먹는 편이에요.
   B: 매운 김치를 먹을 때는 물을 많이 마셔요.

15 A. 어떤 한국음식을 가장 좋아합니까?
   B: 그렇게 맵지 않은 것이 좋아요.

A: 잡채 좋아해요?
B: 물론, 좋아해요.
A: 김치 어때요?
B: 김치는 너무 매워서 그렇게 좋아하지 않아요.

16 B: 초대 받아서 홍과장님 댁에 갔어요.
B: 홍과장님 생신이었어요.
B: 예, 많이 먹었어요.
B: 잡채가 가장 맛있었어요.

17 약속시간을 6시로 알고 너무 빨리 김과장님 댁에 도착했다. 손님이 올 때까지 비디오 영화를 보면서 기다렸고 7시에 재미있는 파티가 시작되었다.

Lesson 18

1 새 아파트로 이사했다면서요?

2 저 건물은 46층이라면서요?

3 새 차와 새 아파트를 사셨다면서요?

4 장선생님은 회의가 끝나자마자 나가셨어요.

5 시청에서 비서로 일하곤 했어요.

6 주말에 친구들과 등산을 가곤 해요.

7 새로 이사했으니까, 한 턱 내겠어요.

8 저희 동네도 마찬가지예요.

9 a Jane은 다음 달에 일본에 갈 모양이에요.
  b 내 동생은 집에 오자마자 화장실에 들어갔다.
  c 여름에 날씨가 더우면, 사람들은 옷을 벗곤 한다.

10 A: 비싼 아파트로 이사 했다면서요? 그것이 사실이에요?
  B: 예, 새 아파트로 이사한지 석달 됐어요.
  A: 아파트가 얼마나 큽니까?
  B: 25평쯤 돼요. 세 식구 살기엔 좋아요.
  A: 아파트 단지의 사람들은 만나봤어요?
  B: 아뇨, 하지만, 집들이에 사람들을 초대할거예요.

A: 집들이 할 때 저도 초대해줘요.
B: 물론이죠!

11 B: 지난 달 말에 갔어요.
 B: 아직 만나지 못했어요.
 B: 시간 나면 초대할까 해요.
 B: 물론이죠.

12 이번 주말에 야유회 갈 시간 없어요.

13 선약이 있어서 쇼핑갈 시간이 없어요.

14 새 차를 살 계획이에요.

15 가구는 아직 새 것처럼 보여요.

16 이번에 그 회의에 참석할 필요가 없어요.

17 새 아파트로 이사한 지 일년 되었어요.

18 백화점 쇼핑도 할 겸, 영화도 볼 겸해서 명동에 갑시다.

19 A: 강남의 새 집으로 이사한지 얼마나 됐어요?
 B: 석달쯤 됐어요.
 A: 집이 모두 정돈됐어요?
 B: 아뇨, 아직 엉망이에요.
 A: 다 정리되면 보여 주세요.
 B: 물론, 그러죠.

20 B: 아니오, 아직 집이 엉망이에요.
 B: 2주 정도 걸릴거예요.
 B: 예, 다음 달에 할까 해요.

21 William Ryan씨는 40평짜리 아파트를 샀는데, 아직 집 정돈이 되지 않아서 회사 직원들을 초대하지 못했다.

Lesson 19

1 지난 주 휴가라서 일하러 가지 않았어요.

2 더운 여름이라서 많은 사람들이 해변에 왔어요.

3 너무 늦게 일어나서 회의에 늦을 뻔 했어요.

4 기름이 다 떨어져서 큰일 날 뻔 했어요.

5 4리터 넣어 주세요.

6 아파서 가지 못했어요.

7 이것은 새 옷이거든요.

8 A: 기름 넣어 드릴까요?
B: 예. 2리터 넣어 주세요.
A: 그럼요. 창을 닦아 드릴까요?
B: 하지 않아도 돼요. 오늘 아침에 청소했거든요.
A: 알겠어요.

9 B: 이 근처에 있는 주유소 아세요?
B: 누구한테 물어 볼까요?
B: 경찰 아저씨, 이 근처에 있는 주유소 아세요?
A and B: 아, 미안합니다.

10 이 세 가지 일을 오늘 오후에 끝내 버립시다.

11 오후 4시에 친구하고 종로에서 만나기로 했어요.

12 기차로 가기로 했어요.

13 저는 서울을 좋아하기는 합니다.

14 그 남자는 일을 잘하기는 합니다만.

15 공원 잔디밭에 들어 가면 안 돼요.

16 그렇게 오래 텔레비젼을 봐서는 안 돼요.

17 회의하는 동안에 세 사람이 전화했어요.

18 제 차가 고장이 난 것 같은데 한번 봐 주시겠어요?

19 아까 달리는데 이상한 소리가 나기는 했어요.

20 A: 어떻게 오셨어요?
B: 제 차가 고장난 것 같아요.

A: 어떤 문제가 있나요?
B: 엔진이 과열된 것 같아요.
A: 점검해 보죠. 아, 냉각수가 모두 다 빠져 버렸군요.

21 B: 어디가 고장 났습니까?
B: 라지에타에서 물이 다 빠져 버렸군요.
B: 4시간 걸립니다.

22 쌘드라씨가 차를 운전할 때 라지에이타의 물이 다 새어 버렸기 때문에 이상한 소리가 나서 차를 고치고 집으로 그냥 돌아왔다.

Lesson 20

1 열이 41도까지 올라간 적도 있어요.

2 전에 그 소설을 읽은 적이 있어요.

3 밤새도록 한 숨도 못 잤어요.

4 그가 전화 받을 수 있는지 물어 보겠어요.

5 할 일이 많이 있어요.

6 죽을 정도로 속이 아파요.

7 눈이 아파서 한 숨도 못 잤어요.

8 a 어제밤에 열이 39도까지 올라간 적이 있어요.
b 응급환자를 받을 수 있는지 물어 볼게요.
c 오늘은 감기 환자가 많이 밀려 있어요.

9 A: 어디가 가장 아프세요?
B: 머리가 아파요.
A: 얼마나 아프죠?
B: 너무 아파서 한 숨도 못 잤어요.
A: 오, 안됐군요. 우선 진찰하도록 합시다.

10 B: 목이 많이 아파요.
B: 목이 부은 것 같아요.
B: 무슨 증상인 것 같아요?

11 목이 아프면서 두통이 심해요.

12 몸이 아파도 오늘 일했어요.

13 세게 눌러도 그렇게 아프지 않아요.

14 체온이 40도까지 올라갔던가요?

15 이과장님이 지금 사무실에 계시던가요?

16 저 건물은 63 빌딩이라고 생각돼요.

17 모두에게 물품을 드릴테니 줄 서세요.

18 a 배를 누르면, 아프지 않던가요?
   b 감기약을 처방해 줄 터이니, 여기서 기다리세요.
   c 요즘 유행하는 독감이라고 생각됩니다.

19 A: 어디가 가장 많이 아프죠?
   B: 고열이 나면서 목이 아파요.
   A: 진찰대 위에 누우시겠어요?
   B: 이렇게 말입니까?
   A: 예. 좋습니다.
   B: 이곳을 누르면 아파요?
   A: 거기는 안 아파요.

20 B: 배가 많이 아파요.
   B: 이렇게 말입니까? (돌아 누우면서)
   B: 배 위쪽이 아픕니다.
   B: 목은 아프지 않습니다.

21 열이 40도까지 오르고 배가 아파서 잠을 잘 수가 없었으나,
   의사가 진찰 후 4시간마다 감기약을 먹으라고 말했다.

Korean–English glossary

English–Korean glossary

Glossary of terms used

Action verb	Verb expressing an action (e.g., "go," "eat")
Adjectival verb	Verb describing or limiting a noun (e.g., "big" 크다 or "big house" 큰 집). Roughly equivalent to an adjective in English
Adverb	A word that modifies a verb (e.g., "quickly"), adjective (e.g., "very bright"), or another adverb (e.g., "very well")
Auxiliary	One of the set of verbs ("can," "may," "must," etc.) subordinate to the lexical verb (e.g., "go")
Case marker	A grammatical marker used to indicate the function of a word in a sentence (e.g., subject case, object case)
Causal conjunction	A term used to indicate a cause-and-effect relationship between two clauses (e.g., "because," "since")
Command	Sentence which gives an order (e.g., "Come here, Jane.")
Comparative	A term used to make a comparison between two objects (e.g., "bigger," "smaller")
Compound	A term used to combine two words into a single word (e.g., "rain" + "fall" = "rainfall")
Conjunction	A word that connects two or more words, phrases, or clauses (e.g., "although," "but")
Consonant	Sound made by a closure or narrowing in the vocal tract (e.g., /k/, /g/)
Contraction	A term used to shorten forms of words (e.g., "he's," "wouldn't")
Coordinate conjunction	A conjunction that connects two main clauses (e.g., "and", "but," "or")
Correlational pattern	Combination of more than two prepositions in sentence structure (e.g., "from ... to")
Declarative	Verb form or sentence/clause used to state a fact (e.g., "John is ill today.")

Demonstrative	Adjective or pronoun indicating the person or thing referred to (e.g., "this," "that")
Dependent clause	Refers to a group of words that contain a subject and a predicate but which depends on the main clause to complete its meaning
Discourse	A continuous stretch of language larger than a sentence
Exclamation	Sentence which expresses the speaker's feelings (e.g., "What a pity!")
Existential verb	Verb expressing existence, sometimes preceded by "there" (e.g., "(there) exists," "located")
Honorific	Word or part of a word used to express levels of politeness or respect, especially in relation to the compared social status of the participants (e.g., "Your Majesty")
Indirect speech	Used of grammatical constructions to report in one's own words what another speaker has said (e.g., "He said he did not go there.")
Interrogative	Type of sentence which asks a question (e.g., "Are you studying Korean?")
Intransitive verb	A verb which cannot take a direct object (e.g., "*He went the egg.")
Linking verb	A verb that describes a condition related to the subject (e.g., "is," "seem," "become")
Main clause	A group of words containing subject and predicate which stands alone as a sentence (e.g., "He is cutting the grass on the field.")
Modifier	A word used in a sentence to qualify the meaning (e.g., "*bad* man")
Negation	Construction that contradicts all or some of a sentence's meaning (e.g., "not," "nobody")
Nominalization	A term used to indicate the process of forming a noun from some other word class (e.g., "his *going* to the theater" – verb to noun)
Noun	Name of a person, a place, thing, or a quality (e.g., "book")
Object	Constituent of the sentence which is the "receiver" or "goal" of the action of the verb (e.g., "He cashed *the check* at the bank.")
Particle	A term use to refer to an element which does not readily fit into parts of speech (e.g., "*to* swim," "I do *not* understand")

Permissive conjunction	Conjunction which expresses being allowed to do something (e.g., "may")
Permissive ending	An ending which permits the action of the verb in a sentence to take place
Possessive	A term used to show ownership (e.g., "his," "my")
Postposition	A word of place and time in Korean which follows a noun (or noun phrase) (e.g., 집 "house" + 에 "to")
Predicate	All remaining parts of the sentence other than the subject ("I *walked to school*")
Progressive	A term used to refer to a contrast of a temporal or durative kind of the verb (e.g., "He *is studying* physics.")
Pronoun	A word used to substitute for the name of a person, place, or thing (e.g., "he," "it")
Relative clause marker	A grammatical element which combines one noun (or noun phrase) with another
Relativization	The process of combining a clause into a noun phrase (e.g., "The man who went was . . .")
Relativize	The process of combining one noun phrase with another
Request	Sentence asking someone to do something (e.g., "Please come here.")
Sentence	A group of words that expresses a complete thought (e.g., "A boy fell into the pond.")
Sino-Korean	Adjective used to refer to words that have originated in Chinese characters and have become Koreanized in their pronounciation
Stative verb	Verb describing a condition which relates only to the subject, expressing a state of affairs rather than an action (e.g., "know," "believe")
Subordinate clause	A group of words that contains a subject and a predicate but depends on the main clause to complete its meaning
Subordinate conjunction	A term used to refer to a word or group of words used to connect a subordinate clause to another part of the sentence (e.g., "although," "since," "after")
Suffix	Additional element added after a root or stem to express grammatical relationships or create new words (e.g., "want*ed*," "internal*ize*")
Superlative	Term used to desribe adjectives or adverbs to express a comparison between more than two entities (e.g., "best," longest)

Temporal conjunction	Conjunction which marks a difference in time (e.g., "after," "before")
Tense	The way grammar marks the time at which the action denoted by the verb took place (e.g., present, past, and future)
Topic	The person or thing about which something is said. In most instances, the topic coincides with the subject of a sentence
Transitive verb	A verb which can take a direct object (e.g., "I saw the film.")
Verb	A word used to describe an action or to state a condition (e.g., "love," "exist")
Verb stem	Root of a verb, except the last syllable (-다) which follows it (e.g., 가- in the verb 가다 "go")
Vowel	Speech sound made without a complete closure in the mouth or a degree of narrowing which would produce audible friction (e.g., /e/, /i/, /u/)

Grammar index

L = Lesson